THE BATTLE FOR
MANCHESTER CITY

THE BATTLE FOR

MANCHESTER
CITY

ALEC JOHNSON

MAINSTREAM
PUBLISHING
EDINBURGH AND LONDON

First published in Great Britain in 1994 by
MAINSTREAM PUBLISHING COMPANY (EDINBURGH) LTD
7 Albany Street
Edinburgh EH1 3UG

ISBN 1 85158 654 7

A catalogue record for this book is available from the British Library

Typeset in ITC-Garamond by Pioneer Associates (Graphic) Ltd
Printed in Great Britain by Butler and Tanner Ltd, Frome

For Sally, Helen, David and Michael

ACKNOWLEDGMENTS

I HAVE received wonderful help from hundreds of former Manchester City players, directors and officials. There are, however, some people who were especially generous in their assistance. I thank Francis Lee and Colin Barlow particularly for their considerations. Others who made my job a lot easier are John Maddocks, that wizard statistician, Peter Gardner, of the *Manchester Evening News*, Ken Barnes, Roy Bailey, Roy Clarke, Ian Ross (*Daily Telegraph*), John Keith (*Daily Express*), Colin Wood (*Daily Mail*), Norman Wynne (*News of the World*), Margaret Carlton and Derek Partridge.

FOREWORD
by Francis Lee

THIS IS Manchester City's Centenary Year, and I am delighted that this book recalls some of the club's finest achievements during the time Joe Mercer was manager. I was privileged to play in that superb side. It was a truly great era during which we won the League Championship, the FA Cup, the League Cup and the European Cup Winners Cup.

There was a burning spirit of comradeship among all who played a part in those days of rich reward—not just among the players who achieved so much on the field, but also in every single member of the Maine Road staff from chairman Albert Alexander right down to the tea ladies. City was one big happy family.

I am especially delighted and honoured to have become Manchester City's new chairman. Since those balmy days of success under Joe Mercer the club has had bitterly disappointing times. It has been a cheerless period of depression for the loyal fans whose patience has been sorely tried. But now I plan, along with the rest of the City directors, to set out to try and bring back those days of success that our wonderful supporters deserve.

There have been some tremendous ups and downs at City over the past 25 years and this book chronicles the drama of it all.

I have known and been good friends with Alec Johnson since he covered my début for Bolton Wanderers as a 16-year-old. In the world of sports journalism, he is a real professional. His book will take the reader through all the roller-coaster times. Best of all, it takes you back to the days when Manchester City was a power in the land. That is how we all want to see the club in the very near future.

PROLOGUE

IT WAS SPRING of 1922 and excitement was in the air for Manchester City supporters. The club were soon to move from their humble Hyde Road headquarters to a magnificent stadium planned to be built in Moss Side. No wonder the Blues supporters were slapping one another on the back and talking of new triumphs to come.

Yet a terrible shadow was to be cast over the Moss Side site long before that famous stadium came into fruition.

City's directors were anxious that the work should be completed as quickly as possible. This was to be the greatest club ground in England—even comparable to Wembley. But as the officials hurried in those early days of planning on the croft and open land that was to be the dream pitch they saw problems. On the far side of the land they were developing stood a group of gypsy caravans. This was no unusual sight in Lancashire. They were not permanent settlers, just trading travellers. Typical of the petty officialdom of the club at that time though, a lackey was sent to tell the gypsies to leave.

The Romanies reacted politely, but insisted they were not permanent residents on the Moss Side site. They would be leaving in a few hours when they had sold their wares. Despite that assurance and only a short time after that first brusque warning, the City official returned to tell the gypsies arrogantly, 'Push off— NOW. We have purchased this land and you are trespassing.'

It was typical of the high-handed City attitude that was to be seen in the years to come. The gypsies had already protested they were merely stationed on the spot for a brief period during which they would be selling their wares. Now this cruel harassment stung them into terrible retaliation. As the City official stood waiting for them to go, a tall, ominous figure faced him from the steps of one of the caravans. He stepped purposely down to the ground. The City official took a few hesitant steps backwards. The gypsy confronted him in chilling tones. 'We have done no harm here. Therefore, hear this. No good will come to anyone who will dwell here.'

One gentleman who remembers this stark piece of City history is Bert Hindson, a great City supporter who lived in Moss Side at that time. He recalls the gypsies vividly. 'They were doing no harm whatsoever,' he told me. 'I heard about the gypsy's curse. They were upset at being told to clear off. They were doing no harm, just trading with the householders in the area. They were selling pegs and the like.

'Me and my little brother played on the croft in the centre of that area. There was a pond and I remember that a toy boat I was playing with suddenly sank like a stone. It must be just about under the penalty spot at the Umbro stand end of the ground.'

Certainly, many people connected with the famous Maine Road club have reason to wonder on those eerie memories of the past. There are others who believe the ground is haunted. Listen to City's former Welsh international winger Roy Clarke, who enjoyed a successful career in the late 1940s and 1950s.

'According to a story, there was a quarry where the City ground now stands. There was a deep pool and a man with a horse and cart slid into it and drowned. He has been seen many times over the years at certain points on the ground. The tea ladies call him Fred. There is certainly something strange and quite inexplicable about the place. Time without number, a door has been heard banging monotonously in the North Stand. Yet the moment someone has gone across to see what is causing it, the sound stops abruptly.

'There is another weird business. Our groundsman Stan Gibson had a huge Alsatian. It could be quite aggressive and I was very wary of it. But whenever Stan would walk with it towards the H Block end the dog would dig its heels in just before he reached it and its fur would bristle. It was quite frightening.

'A figure has been seen in the foyer of the club on countless occasions, but the secretaries in the reception area say that the

12

minute they look at him the figure disappears into thin air.

'There was something out on the pitch also that was quite inexplicable. During a match, even on a warm afternoon, I would be darting down the wing when suddenly I would find myself in a current of freezing cold air. It was quite extraordinary and there seemed no explanation for the severe change in temperature. It made you shiver.'

A City curse . . . a City ghost . . . whatever you may make of those stories, one thing is for certain—over the years Maine Road has had more than its share of bad luck as well as its successes.

CHAPTER ONE

JOE MERCER and Malcolm Allison faced one another angrily, eyes blazing. One of the great manager-coach partnerships of English football was breaking up and those who witnessed it could hardly believe their ears. The normally bluff Mercer rounded on his flamboyant protégé whom he now regarded as the man out to destroy his Manchester City dream.

'I brought you to Maine Road from off the scrap-heap,' bellowed Mercer.

Allison's eyes were hard as he retorted angrily, 'I put you where you are today. You wouldn't have won any of your trophies but for me.'

This bitter row, on 11 December 1971, spilled over in the hotel bar in Malta where City had flown out for a friendly match against Floriana. There had been no hint earlier that Saturday of the drama that would tear apart the marvellous Mercer-Allison partnership. Their fascinating combination of guile and devilry had set English soccer alight. It had seen City rise from a humiliating, lowly position in the Second Division to football glory. They had swept off with the First Division Championship, the FA Cup, the League Cup and European Cup Winners Cup. Back at Maine Road before they flew out of Ringway that same fateful Saturday, City had beaten Ipswich 4-0 at Maine Road, with goals from Colin Bell, Francis Lee, Wyn Davies and Ian Mellor.

But on that night, on the flight out to Malta, something that had been smouldering between the wily Mercer and his brilliant coach

15

flared up. Allison wanted to be manager in his own right. He felt he had served Mercer loyally and now he was entitled to tell the grand old King it was time to leave the throne. But Mercer wasn't going to give up the crown without a fight. Embarrassed directors and players moved away as more angry words were exchanged between the former close friends.

Eric Alexander, chairman of the club at that time, knew that this confrontation marked the end of a wonderful relationship. But what neither he nor anyone else at Maine Road could ever have realised was what the breaking up of this superb alliance would mean to City over the next 20 years.

Any hope that the flare-up between the management pals might have been one of those unhappy incidents that happen in the heat of the moment during the tension of a hard season was rapidly dispelled the next day when chairman Alexander and other directors heard another bitter quarrel going on between Mercer and Allison as the City party went for a stroll in Valetta. Allison was heard to snap at Mercer, 'I could have done the whole thing on my own.' An angry Mercer later turned to his chairman and said, 'He reckons he could have done it on his own.'

The players were numbed by the bitter split between the two, and one player predicted to the others, 'From here on it is all going to be downhill . . . it's the end of the road for Manchester City.'

But if most of the players and several of the directors were alarmed at the turn of events, several members of the board welcomed the showdown Allison had set in motion, for not only was this a time of struggle for power in the manager's office, it also heralded an even more ruthless and bitter battle in the boardroom for control of the club itself.

It was to be a moment in Manchester City's history when most people closely involved with the famous Maine Road club believed it was on its way up the creek without a paddle—and they will say so quite bluntly as our story unfolds.

Chairman Alexander was determined to try to halt the savage rift between Mercer and his protégé. 'I knew that a certain faction on the board were pushing for Malcolm to be given his head,' he told me. 'I was determined to stand by Joe. Maybe it was the time for a younger man to get his chance, but there was a right way to do it. I wanted this partnership that had done so much for us to continue. Okay, Malcolm should be given the title of manager that he craved for, but I was determined Joe's wisdom and guiding hand should be there to steady things.'

Alexander acknowledges Allison had a point. 'When Joe became manager, he insisted he only wanted the job for a few short years. He took Malcolm from the obscurity of Plymouth and gave him a wonderful chance to show what a great coach he was. But Joe had said to us originally that he wanted a younger man to eventually take over, and that man was clearly Malcolm. Yet in my opinion, even with Malcolm appointed manager, it was vital to keep Joe's vital influence.' Alexander was certain in his own mind that 'Joe was worth his weight in gold' at Maine Road. His presence at Allison's side to guide him expertly round the minefields of soccer management would be vital.

The board finally agreed that Joe should be given the chance to stay, though with a new title. Yet when it was put as tactfully as possible to Mercer by Alexander that the board felt it was time for him to hand over the reins to Allison, the old war-horse snorted with indignation. He stomped into the office of former City skipper and then coach Ken Barnes and blurted out, 'They want to switch me upstairs . . . make me into a sort of general manager. That's no good for me. I want to be out with the players, and with them in the dressing-room.'

Nothing would pacify him. No matter how much Barnes and the rest of the staff tried, Joe could not accept that it was time to let go of the reins of management. Alexander paid an early morning call at Mercer's house and told him that the board wanted him to decide on what his new title should be, provided it didn't contain the word 'manager'. The City chairman was confident his plan of keeping Joe on as a vital guiding hand on Malcolm was going to work.

'Thank you very much for coming to see me,' replied Mercer, politely promising to give his verdict in a few days time. Yet Mercer was a bitter man and a few days later when Alexander was boarding a boat in the Isle of Man to return to Manchester after a weekend break, he was stopped in his tracks by a banner headline on the sports page in a newspaper. It read: 'Mercer New Coventry City Manager.'

Says Alexander, 'I was thunderstruck. I couldn't believe that Joe would do such a thing. I'd stuck my neck out for him and yet he just walked out on us. It certainly cost me dearly. Shortly afterwards, a takeover group got control in the boardroom and I eventually quit the chairmanship.'

Mercer said of the parting, 'The humiliating part of this sad affair was that at one time the board was saying there was a job for life. But the new régime of directors had no real confidence in me. The thing that hurt most of all was that they just didn't know what to call me. All my life I had been known as Joe Mercer the footballer or Joe Mercer the manager. Then suddenly they can't find a title for me. That was when my pride was hit most of all.'

Since that sad exit of Mercer, City have constantly been second best to Manchester United. If you are a City fan, that may hurt—but it is true. Even when United sank for one humbling season into the Second Division, they still bounced back to the big time the next season under the flamboyant managership of Tommy Docherty. How did City get into the humiliating position of appointing 14 managers since Mercer's sad exit and only have one trophy to show in all that time . . . the League Cup?

To answer that question we must go back to when it was decided in the boardroom that it was time for Joe to move over and give Malcolm his big chance. As his loyal players watched incredulously at the turn of events that led to fatherly Joe's exit and Malcolm's rise to power, there was some alarm. Mike Summerbee, the fleet-footed winger with a bubbling sense of fun and a mesmerising ability to turn defences inside out, was horrified at this turn of events. 'The decision to allow Joe Mercer to be pushed to one side as manager of our club was the biggest disaster ever to happen to Manchester City,' he maintains. 'The club has suffered ever since that day. It has meant that all the plans Joe had to build up a truly impressive squad such as United had across the way had gone. Joe was a fraction away from making City finally and completely the number one club in Manchester. Once Joe had gone the whole City castle fell to pieces. You had to have the leadership of Joe Mercer. The players loved him. He was a father to them.

'When we heard Joe was to be replaced as manager by Malcolm, we were stunned.' Together, Joe and Malcolm had been peaches and cream. 'We knew that when Joe was removed from Malcolm's side, he would never have the polish for the job as manager.

'I think every player at City was worried when they heard Joe was to step down as manager. They knew it was the end of a won-derful adventure, yet it was hard to take in. Malcolm had been an inspiration as a coach. But without Joe it was never to be the same again. Most of all, we knew in our heart of hearts that we had lost our leader.'

Summerbee has no doubts about the tragedy of the break-up of the winning partnership. He says, 'Joe simply loved the challenge of the job. He was confident we had quite a few more years of success. He wanted to win the European Cup and we could well have done it if he had stayed.'

Summerbee is the first to laud Allison's genius as a coach but insists, 'There is a lot of difference between the two positions, and Malcolm's role was on the field coaching, not sitting in the manager's office where all the politics go on.'

Mercer told some of the City players sadly, 'I always wanted Malcolm to have the job eventually. But at the same time I wanted to retain some control . . . to help him along the way.' But this relationship couldn't work unless it was on a mutual understanding. 'There was no way I wanted to stay around unless I still had some authority, but they just didn't see it my way. I am heartbroken at the way it has all worked out.'

So, at the age of 58, Joe Mercer and Manchester City Football Club had reached the parting of the ways. He left bitterly hurt, insisting he still had a major role to play in the club's future.

Tony Book, City's superb skipper in those Mercer-Allison glory years, gives his verdict on Mercer's sad exit. Book, who has since proved the best manager of the club since Mercer, has no doubts that losing Mercer was a blunder that cost City dearly. 'I could see at that time that Malcolm wanted to move into the manager's chair. But giving him the job and subsequently losing Joe was a great mistake for the club,' says Book. 'Malcolm was a truly brilliant coach—there is absolutely no doubt about that and especially at that particular time with City. With Joe running the management side, Malcolm was perfect to work with the players, and in training it was marvellous.

'But Malcolm was NOT the man for management and I think he probably realised it was a mistake himself quite soon after Joe had left. Joe felt he still had more to achieve and I agree that we could have won more trophies if he had stayed and if we had continued as we were. It was very sad that it should all end like that.'

City fans were to realise bitterly in the long, unhappy ensuing years that they were in for a lean time. Yet not even the most pessimistic punter could have known how utterly depressing the future was going to prove. But before we take a hard, critical look at those long, bleak years since Joe's departure, let us go back. Back to the moment when Mercer arrived at City, when they were struggling in the lower reaches of the Second Division. We will relive those stunning years which Mercer produced like a Merlin of soccer. But we will also learn how things went desperately wrong for a great club, a club of such superb pedigree.

CHAPTER TWO

GLOOM HUNG OVER Maine Road. It was Easter 1965 and manager George Poyser had just resigned after two seasons of rank disappointment. Poyser, who had taken over when Les McDowall was sacked in 1963. Poyser, a former Wolverhampton Wanderers, Port Vale and Plymouth player who had been assistant to McDowall and had been in charge of City's scouting system. Poyser, who never had the flair nor the vital ability to inspire a Second Division City team to reach the promotion form to get them back into the top flight where the fans were demanding they should be.

He seemed to be on the right lines in his first season as City's new boss. Poyser brought in new blood. He signed the bustling goal-grabber Derek Kevan, from Chelsea, for £35,000 and then Jimmy Murray, from his old club Wolves, for £27,500. Those were princely sums to pay in those days. In his second season he signed Dave Bacuzzi from Arsenal for £14,000. Then came an inspired signing with the arrival of the exciting John Crossan from Sunderland for a whopping £40,000. He also sold winger David Wagstaffe to Wolves for £44,750. But City slid halfway down the Second Division table and the League gates slumped alarmingly. Poyser quit.

Board chairman at this point was little Albert Alexander, a shrewd, loveable man who had played for the City 'A' team. He was determined not to rush into a reckless appointment. His son Eric Alexander, who later joined the board of directors and was to follow in his father's footsteps, said, 'My father wanted to get a man with a chosen pedigree.'

If Manchester City had any qualms about their standing in the British soccer scene, then two of the first applicants to come panting to their door soon made them realise that the Maine Road 'hot seat' had a special appeal.

One was none other than the famous Bill Shankly, then proving a highly successful manager of Liverpool. The gravel-voiced Scot with a wonderful, gritty sense of humour had been a brilliant midfield player with Preston North End and Scotland. At Deepdale he had played behind the legendary North End and England winger, Tom Finney. Certainly Finney was not surprised at Shankly's emergence into successful soccer managership. 'He had a tremendous brain for the game and was fascinated by tactics, but basically Bill could see a player's value to a team instinctively. He was a tremendous character and quite inspirational.' Shankly certainly saw the City job as maybe an even greater challenge than the one at Anfield. Equally it was a time when managers were certainly not on the massive salaries offered in today's big business world of football. Quite understandably, Shankly would be hoping to be offered a more lucrative contract by the move to Maine Road.

Another applicant for the chance to lead City back to greatness was former Maine Road favourite, Don Revie, who was then manager at Leeds United. Revie had begun his career as a player with Leicester City although he was born in Middlesbrough. He then moved to Hull City before joining Manchester City for £25,000 in 1951. He had played in the two FA Cup finals, first in 1955 when City lost 3-1 to Newcastle United and in 1956 when City lifted the trophy after beating Birmingham City 3-1. A great tactician, Revie was proving to be an impressive manager at Leeds and he was a formidable candidate for City's board to consider.

'Nobody had any idea that Shankly and Revie wanted a crack at a chance with us,' reveals Eric Alexander.

Recalling the period, he says, 'I think a lot of chairmen would have taken one of them aboard straightaway, but my father and a majority of the other directors were interested in having a go for Joe Mercer.'

At that time, a move for Mercer with two men like Shankly and Revie waiting in the wings hoping for their cue seemed positively crazy, for Mercer was an ill man. After an illustrious career with Everton and then Arsenal, during which he won three League Championship medals and FA Cup winners medals, he was forced

22

to quit after breaking a leg during a game. He had moved into soccer management. His first spell was with Sheffield United where he impressed with the quality of the football his team played. Then he had moved on to Aston Villa. Here the Mercer success ship suddenly hit the rocks. He guided Villa, winning them promotion to the First Division and then the League Cup. But the pressure was too much—he quit through poor health.

He was suffering from hypertension and had been ordered complete bed rest by the doctors. When City approached, they were warned that if Joe was brought back into football, it might be the end of him. His loyal wife, Norah, tried her best to dissuade him from considering making a comeback but Joe felt that the only answer to his problem was to take up the challenge of the City offer. He told City's emissary, 'The simple matter is this: football can do without Joe Mercer, but I can't do without football. I shall take the job. It is the only way I can go on enjoying my life. Without soccer my life isn't worth living.'

City's directors and their supporters were elated—and rightly so. Never in their wildest dreams could they have foreseen what lay ahead—seven years of pure heaven as Mercer waved his magic wand to transform the struggling Second Division club into possibly the most exciting and celebrated football team in the whole of its existence. It wasn't just the fact that City won things—it was the dazzling style in which they beat their opponents.

Across at Old Trafford, Matt Busby's mighty United side glittered with stars. The incomparable Bobby Charlton, the peerless Denis Law and the enigmatic George Best held court. The City fans had been wriggling in embarrassment as United lifted the trophies with monotonous regularity. But City were to frighten the life of that great Busby team. At City's height in Mercer's great era, many critics called for the entire City forward line to be picked for England. But that will come later. Mercer's arrival was like a breath of fresh air in the Maine Road corridor.

'It was a difficult time before Mercer came,' says Eric Alexander. 'United were the team everyone talked about and City were just the poor relations. But my father and Joe hit it off right from the start. It was a wonderful atmosphere. Everyone seemed to have a new spring in their stride. There was optimism in the air.'

When it came to optimism, another man was to come to Mercer's side who would be the biggest extrovert and most flamboyant figure ever to hit football. Ironically, the City players had only recently had a taste of what Mercer's new right-hand man was like. In a game at Plymouth in November 1964 the referee awarded a penalty to Plymouth. Skipper John Newman took the kick. But instead of shooting he tapped the ball to his right and Mike Trebilcock darted into the box to blast the ball past the startled 'keeper Alan Ogley. The referee acknowledged the ploy was within the rules and pointed to the centre spot, signifying a numbing goal. The bemused City players then saw a huge figure rise on the touchline and let out a mighty bellow of triumph.

It was the City players' first look at Malcolm Allison in action.

CHAPTER THREE

THE SHREWD MERCER had long been an admirer of the ebullient Allison. He was bowled over by the burning enthusiasm of the former West Ham player whose career had been cut short cruelly when he had to have a chest operation. That was in 1958 and when big Mal got out he was determined the operation wasn't going to stop him making a successful career as a coach or eventually a manager. Yet when Mercer moved for him in 1965 Malcolm had broken with Argyle and was a free agent. Mercer had a firm conviction that Allison was the man he wanted, but knew he had already been approached by another club. The big City adventure for these two highly talented men hung in the balance at that point.

Allison reveals that he and Mercer had first met at the Lilleshall FA soccer centre. 'I was still a player with West Ham at the time,' he says. 'I was on a course with Stanley Matthews, Stan Mortensen and Jimmy Hagan. I was busy practising at swerving the ball. Joe was just kind of looking around. I think he was managing Sheffield United at the time. He watched me with interest and then told me, "You should practise kicking a ball straight, properly, before you start trying to swerve it." '

That story isn't only amusing—it goes a long way to revealing the secret of the magic mixture of Joe and Malcolm. Allison was always experimenting, reaching out for new ideas to implement. But Joe was always to be at his side to bring him back to basics and keep his feet on the ground. The two complemented each other. Allison had been a great believer in England team boss Walter Winterbottom.

He would talk football tactics as long as there was anyone to listen—and he always had a rapt audience when his team-mates used to meet him in a restaurant near West Ham's ground in their playing days.

Recalling his decision to join Mercer at Maine Road, Allison says, 'I had had a row with the Plymouth Argyle directors. I had a call from Raich Carter, the manager of Middlesbrough, asking me to come up and talk about joining him as coach. I told Joe that Carter wanted me but he said, "Please come and see me first." I was impressed by Joe and the City set-up. Manchester has always been a big soccer city, especially with United across the road and being dominant. It was a challenge. So I joined them for the princely sum of £50 per week as first team coach. By Christmas we were second in the Division Two table, so I got a £10 a week rise.'

'When Allison arrived, everyone at the ground was captivated,' said Eric Alexander. 'He was a larger-than-life character and nothing seemed to daunt him. You could see the electricity Mercer and Allison generated between them. I don't think anyone doubted they were going to do big things. But the speed of their success was quite phenomenal.'

Now at City the entire squad, from the experienced first-teamers down to the most starry-eyed junior, paid strict attention to what Allison had to say—and loved it. Here was the perfect partnership. The jocular yet witty, sage Mercer flanked by the big, brash coach Allison for whom they were all ready to run through the nearest brick wall if necessary.

'You have the word motivate used so often in football,' says Francis Lee. 'Well, Malcolm Allison was the biggest motivator I have ever heard in my entire career in soccer.'

But there was an extra dimension to Allison's usefulness to Manchester City. In all my 27 years covering the magnificent Manchester soccer scene for the *Daily Mirror*, I have never known anyone to match Malcolm for knowing how to grab the headlines and hold the spotlight on himself, Joe and the club. He was the master of public relations. Whenever you trotted into his and Joe's office, there was almost always the pop of a champagne cork and an early bottle of bubbly for the press men awaiting the write-up on City's battle plans for Saturday's game.

It was the perfect ploy. Press men are renowned for their love of a good drink and Malcolm played on it with alacrity. We might have returned to our offices a little light-headed, but almost inevitably we had a back page splash story provided by Malcolm and Joe. It was this effortless repartee between Joe and Malcolm and the press that did so much to build up City's great image during that period and to set them up alongside Matt Busby's United.

Joe and Malcolm out-foxed Busby in that field. For Busby, although extremely affable with the newspapermen, was always inclined to keep his cards close to his chest. If you rang Malcolm and asked him if anything was happening, he would often say, 'Well, not right now, but I'll go and have a chat with Joe and we'll think of something.' Fifteen minutes later, Allison would be telling you some quite extraordinary yarn such as when he announced that he was getting a psychiatrist into the dressing-room to help the team. City certainly didn't need a psychiatrist when they had the voluble Malcolm Allison to inspire them to unbelievable heights.

Allison loved a gamble and is reputed on one occasion to have won £10,000 on a horse bet—and remember we are talking back in the '60s. He certainly got some incredible tips. Once, at the Friday morning press conference, Malcolm puffed on a huge cigar and told us to back a horse in the Hennessy Gold Cup. It sounded like a crazy bet as the horse was a 40-1 long shot. A good friend of mine, Peter Keeling, the former great international athletics star and a hard-working freelance sports writer, was always ready to put up a good stake if he felt it was worth his while. He heard of Malcolm's tip but half an hour before the race decided against his previous decision to put a couple of hundred pounds on it. Before the game at Bolton Wanderers that we were covering on the day of the race, Peter went to watch the horses on television in the supporters' club lounge. Just before the kick-off he emerged in the press box looking horror-struck. 'Was it anywhere?' I asked. 'It won by a head at 40-1!' was the strangled reply from Peter. I know that most of Manchester City's lads were on Malcolm's tip and must have had a field day.

Certainly Joe and Malcolm got it right on the field in their first season together. Playing with a fresh abandon that thrilled the fans, City stormed to promotion, winning the Second Division championship in 1965-66 season.

It was this panache which the Mercer-Allison liaison brought to Maine Road that excited the fans. 'Joe and Malcolm clicked right away,' says Alexander. 'But we quickly got used to Malcolm's lavish lifestyle when the bills started to roll in for the champagne and cigars. My dad used to say, "Oh Malcolm, what's all this—not another bloody bill?" But Malcolm would just give him a big grin and say, "That was a little relaxation in between winning things for you." And we would all laugh and just shrug and say, "That's Malcolm."'

It was only a small price to pay as far as Albert Alexander and his directors were concerned. They knew they had a top management partnership in Joe and Malcolm that would surely be able to challenge the great Matt Busby and Jimmy Murphy union at Old Trafford.

Ken Barnes, the former great City midfield man of the '50s, was a coach and recalls how Malcolm was already anxious to try out some of his winning schemes. 'But Joe was always the steadying influence. Malcolm was doing a great job as first-team coach, but it was Joe who was managing the whole outfit,' Ken told me. 'He would be firm and say, "No, we can't try that system or that plan." Joe wanted the players to express themselves naturally and they reacted superbly for him.'

Glyn Pardoe, the speedy full-back who played such a granite role during all the triumphs of the Mercer-Allison era recalls, 'It was terrific fun both on and off the park. They built up the perfect family atmosphere. There were no stars . . . just players who were big buddies and all out to win as much as they could. With Malcolm you sometimes got the feeling there wasn't anything we couldn't win. He would come bowling into the dressing-room before a game, shouting instructions and pulling people's legs. He just wouldn't allow tension to build up.

'Joe was a genial, jolly boss who had the knack of knowing just how to put his finger on the right spot where we had to concentrate to win a match. He had the final word and it counted! But Joe and Malcolm were a superb team. Malcolm was terrific fun when a game was over. Malcolm on the town had to be seen to be believed. When the work was done he knew how to enjoy himself and wanted us to do the same. He had a tremendous sense of fun in those days and loved to take the mickey. He once asked United's assistant manager Jimmy Murphy if he wanted the loan of some of our reserve players!'

Just before the start of City's return to the big time with the 1966-67 season in the First Division, Mercer and Allison made an extremely important signing, although when the man arrived at

Maine Road from Plymouth Argyle many eyebrows were lifted—it was Tony Book, who was 32! Yet Book was to be one of the most extraordinary success stories in football.

Allison had played the major role in developing Book's career. It was a remarkable story. Allison had been impressed by full-back Book when he had him at Bath City where Allison was manager. 'He was only a part-timer,' recalls Allison, 'and was a brick builder by trade. He had a smashing disposition and I couldn't believe how such a talented defender could have been missed by the rest of the professional game.

'He was quick and had great timing, although he was inclined to be a little reckless with his tackles. I took him to Canada on a tour. Nigel Sims, the top-class Aston Villa 'keeper, saw Tony playing and said he was the best full-back he had ever played with.

'When I left Bath City and joined Plymouth, I signed him for Argyle for £3,000. The directors nearly had a fit when they asked how old he was and I told them he was 28. Actually, he was 30! But he proved he was a bargain buy. Then, when I was with City two years later, Joe and I were looking for a good full-back. Joe sent me to watch three internationals. I was disappointed and went back and told Joe that Tony would be better.'

But Joe insisted that at the age of 32, Book was 'past it' as far as professional football was concerned—especially in the First Division. He had played right into Allison's hands, though, for Malcolm retorted, 'When you were transferred from Everton to Arsenal, were you finished?'

'Of course not,' snorted Mercer.

'Well, you were almost 33 and you went on playing until you were 39 years old,' replied Allison.

Joe realised he had walked into a trap and that was that. It settled the Book deal and they signed him. The rest is soccer history and Book captained the City side to its string of amazing triumphs, as well as winning Player of the Year jointly with Dave Mackay, at the age of 35. It was a truly remarkable performance. What would he have won if he had come into the professional game as a youngster?

Book recalls his meeting with Mercer prior to travelling to Manchester to sign the transfer papers. 'Joe had been to London for a World Cup game and he took me on the tube to catch the main train back to Manchester. In those days managers were very wary of the press and by sheer coincidence a London sports reporter spotted Joe and came over on to the platform. Joe just introduced me as a friend and the reporter went off none the wiser.'

The ice-cool Book was the ideal skipper of this team, packed not only with talent but with a burning ambition to win and win. 'It was a wonderful feeling for me at the ripe old age of 32 to find myself among this wonderful gang of players,' he recalls. 'Joe was a fabulous man. He was incredible considering he still wasn't a completely fit man, as he still suffered from hypertension. But he had charming style. He was a great press relations man. He brought out the very best in players because when they listened to Joe, they realised he had played with flair. Joe wanted them to show that same flair for him, and they did.'

Another important arrival was the superb Colin Bell, signed for £45,000 from Bury. Bell, destined to become a great England star, impressed from the word go, with his flowing runs and subtle control of the ball. His sheer power in those fierce bursts of speed earned him the nickname 'Nijinsky' after the famous racehorse.

Allison was quickly captivated at the sight of Bell in action at nearby Bury. 'He was tall and elegant and when I saw him gliding over the surface of the pitch, I was reminded of the same craft as Peter Doherty, the former great City and Irish player who was one of my idols,' says Allison. 'I kept pestering Joe to sign him. But we knew it would cost around £40,000 to get him and City were not quick to splash out that kind of cash unless we had a real winner. I was convinced we had one of the great players of the future in Colin.

'I kept going over to Bury to watch him.' By now there was a posse of scouts also running the rule over the exciting 18-year-old. 'I was terrified they were going to get in before me,' says Allison. 'So I started running him down and saying to the others, "He's not quick enough . . . he's out of position" . . . anything to try to put doubts in their minds.'

Eventually, Joe persuaded the City board to cough up the £45,000 required to bring Bell to Maine Road. Malcolm was exultant. 'I was absolutely certain we had landed a truly great talent,' he remembers. 'I thought he was unbelievably cheap at the price.' But the wary Joe was still a little sceptical.

Bell, quiet and a little shy on his arrival at Maine Road, was given his début against Derby County at the Baseball Ground on 19 March 1966. 'Colin didn't make much of an impact in the early stages of the game,' recalls Allison. 'In fact, he looked decidedly uncomfortable. Maybe it was just nerves. But Joe was mumbling at my side, "What have you let me in for?" I told him to relax and wait to see the real Colin. Then their goalkeeper hit his clearance against the seat of Colin's pants and the ball flew into the net for a goal. In a flash, I rounded on Joe and yelled, "There you are! I told you the lad was a genius!" '

The third player to arrive and complete the City picture was the stocky, livewire forward Francis Lee, from Bolton Wanderers. Lee had already impressed the soccer world with his powerful play on the wing with the Wanderers. His strength enabled him to score great goals and he had linked well with the legendary striker Nat Lofthouse who at the time told me, 'Francis is so brave and strong. He is ready to listen and learn all the time. That is his greatest attribute. He wants to get better and better.' After making his début at the tender age of 16, Lee was developing into the complete footballer. Luckily for Mercer and Allison, in the 1966-67 season, Lee was unhappy with things at Burnden Park and was anxious to try his luck elsewhere.

Both Mercer and Allison were sure that if they could add Lee to their squad, then they would really be ready to take on anybody in football. He was the final link in the chain. 'We knew if we could get Franny then we would be a power to be reckoned with,' says Allison.

'I first saw Franny when he was just a kid,' recalls Allison. 'I was manager of Bath City and we drew Bolton in the FA Cup. Everything about him impressed me. Most of all it was the confidence—almost a cockiness about him. He seemed to be unafraid of any situation. He would take anyone on and usually won. We were winning 1-0 with only seven minutes to go. Then they had a penalty and they gave the ball to Franny. Although only 17, he just stuck it on the spot. Despite all the Bolton players looking frozen with tension, he just trotted up and whacked the ball home without batting an eyelid. He had that presence about him.'

Joe and Malcolm already had the idea of turning Lee into a centre-forward. 'Most of all we wanted to see him playing alongside Mike Summerbee,' says Allison. 'We weren't sure if we would try Mike in the middle with Franny on the wing, or the other way round. But we reckoned in the same forward line they would be one hell of a pair.'

Allison was given permission to talk to Lee by Bolton and went across to Burnden Park for a chat. Lee was sitting in the social club with his business partner. He had already built up a string of successful businesses which also impressed Allison. 'I'd love you to come and play for Manchester City,' said Allison.

Lee wasn't exactly jumping at the chance. 'It might be interesting,' was his initial reaction.

After an hour of getting nowhere, Allison snapped at Lee, 'You haven't done anything in the game yet. You come to Manchester City and I'll make you a great player.'

After Allison had gone, Lee said to his partner, 'What a big-headed bastard that Allison is.' But Allison had impressed him and Lee went over to see Mercer.

Says Lee today, recalling his first meeting with Joe, 'He told me they had a team that was determined they would win things. At the time I thought it was just the usual blather any manager gives a new player they want to sign for them. But I quickly realised that Joe and Malcolm really meant it. They were determined to be winners—and quickly. It was going to be one hell of an adventure for all of us. Just thinking back to all those tremendous days makes me tingle. It was an unforgettable time for everybody connected with the club.'

City finished a creditable 15th in their first season back with the big boys of the First Division and had a great run in the FA Cup before being beaten 1-0 at Elland Road, by Leeds United, in the sixth round. But despite the dash and style this City team was showing, no one could have been prepared for their extraordinary and electrifying performance in only their second season back in the top flight.

CHAPTER FOUR

IT WAS the mercurial Denis Law, who was dazzling the United fans across at Old Trafford with flashes of sheer wizardry, who saw the signs during the early part of the 1967-68 season that City were a really exciting outfit. He felt there was an especially impressive look about the team.

After a year in Italian football with crack Italian club Torino, who had bought him from City for £110,000, Law had returned to this country and signed for United for £115,000. Law was not only one of the most talented players in the world but he also recognised talent when he saw it. 'Those days in the '60s were fantastic in Manchester,' says the former Scottish international. 'I could see the way City were developing. I knew we were in for some real competition and were going to have great battles from those boys across at Maine Road where I had so many wonderful memories from my days as a City player.

'The whole of Lancashire was having an exciting time with Everton and Liverpool building powerful teams. But the emergence of City under Mercer and Allison was quite remarkable. Joe and Malcolm did it all so quickly. They just burst out of the Second Division and then after one brief season strengthening the side they simply took off. But I could see they had so many really talented players. There was class in players like Colin Bell, Francis Lee, Mike Summerbee, Tony Book, Alan Oakes, Mike Doyle and all the rest of them. They played for one another. It was a real TEAM. Some of the derby matches we had with them were quite unforgettable.'

City were gaining in strength in every sense of the word, for Allison decided, with Joe's blessing, that the players' sheer physical stamina must be built up to a new peak of power. Allison was convinced that top men in other fields of sport could play a key role in helping his squad reach super-fitness. 'I was determined we were going to have the best-conditioned team in the country, if not the world,' says Allison. 'Joe was fascinated, for he had always been a great believer in footballers being in the best physical shape.' Allison went for talks with Dr Brooks, a specialist in physical training at Salford University. 'We decided on a revolutionary plan for a football club,' says Allison. 'We drew up a power scheme. The plan was to make our players so durable they would be capable of outstaying any opposition. It was an enthralling time for everybody involved. And remember that it played a major role in what we were to achieve in the coming season—which was quite fantastic by any standard.'

Allison, with Mercer's backing, drew up a strategy in which two big names from the world of athletics were brought in to make City's players the supermen of the soccer world. They were the famous British miler, Derek Ibbotson, and the cross-country ace, Joe Lancaster. It was a fascinating idea. Here were two men who had mastered the art of staying the pace and knowing how to suddenly put the foot on the pedal with a call to hidden resources of power. Within weeks City players were on the rack of pain as they went through the tortuous plans set up by the two great athletes. Mercer and Allison were elated at the results. Says Allison, 'We had a power scheme. It was as simple as that. But the players had to go through a lot of physical pressure some might have felt was unfair for a professional footballer. Yet there was never a grumble—and it worked brilliantly. The work hurt them at first but they gritted their teeth and went through it.'

Allison also organised a massive training stint involving weights, with a machine that really tested the players' physical powers. City players suddenly felt ready to climb Mount Everest, swim the Channel and then take the League Championship as well. The plan was paying off. Says Allison, 'The players were fabulous. They would even come in early and then stay late for training. The fans were unbelievable at this point. It was like a kind of crusade. Everyone felt we were on our way to something wonderful.'

People were astounded at City's capacity to produce football of the highest calibre and play a never-ending flow of power—right to the final whistle. Allison was bubbling with enthusiasm for the way things were going and Joe Mercer said, 'Now we are ready to go for it, Malcolm. We are on our way.' Says Allison, 'That training was extremely hard work for the players. But it did them so much good in both ways.' Far from shrinking from this grilling set by Allison's panel of perfectionists, the players went for the agonising training plans in a big way. 'It was incredibly hard work for them,' says Malcolm. 'Joe and I wondered if they might feel it was too much to ask. Not a bit of it. When they even came in early for training, that was the big moment for us. It was the sure sign that they had developed self-motivation. They were determined to be winners.'

By now City had signed another great character in left-winger Tony Coleman from Doncaster Rovers. The Liverpool-born Coleman already had a reputation as being a real rebel and very tough to handle. Manager Joe Mercer didn't fancy him one bit when Allison said they should sign him. 'Joe had seen him up to all sorts of tricks at Lilleshall training centre,' Allison told me. 'Of course his tattoos and his crew hairstyle didn't endear him to Joe one little bit. Joe was adamant we would be buying nothing but trouble. So I had to promise Joe I would handle him. But I told him the one thing that mattered most regarding Coleman was that he was a hell of a good player with a tremendous heart. He was an absolute toughie. He was exactly what our team needed at that moment. He was a natural winger with lots of skill and he could get goals as well. In the end, Joe shook his head and said, "Alright, we'll get him. But it's up to you, Mal, to keep him under control." Sure, he was a difficult lad to handle. He did blow up now and then and get himself in hot water. But nevertheless he did the job on the field for us. That was the most important thing. I was pretty proud of that signing, because everyone said we were crazy to get him. But when Tony started to rip defences apart and set up lots of goals they realised that he was a brilliant signing.'

One player who had slipped through City's fingers was Leicester City's great goalkeeper Gordon Banks. 'We could have got him for £50,000,' reveals Malcolm. 'I told Joe to ring Leicester and sew the deal up. He would have been ideal at that figure . . . a gift and what a hell of a 'keeper. But Joe tried to get him cheaper and only offered something around £40,000. Stoke City nipped in and got him for £50,000. What a snip! I was livid to think we had missed a goalkeeper with the ability of Banks and all because of a little amount like £10,000. I felt bitterly disappointed to have missed out on such a great player.'

Yet now Mercer and Allison had assembled a team with more all-round strength. That was why Malcolm said, 'The balance was right. We felt we could have a real go for the championship. What I loved most about that season was the fact that we knew we were going to have to lick Manchester United more than anyone if we were to take the title. They looked the one team who would give us the closest run.' Allison could not have been more right. Ken Mulhearn was in goal, skipper Tony Book and Glyn Pardoe were the full-backs. The powerful Mike Doyle, that dreadnought of the midfield, flanked strong centre-half George Heslop with teak-tough Alan Oakes on Heslop's left. The front line in that season had Franny Lee on the right wing, Colin Bell inside-right, Mike Summerbee at centre-forward with Neil Young and Tony Coleman forming the left wing. A formidable force. The race for the title was on.

So City completed their final plans for the fascinating drive for the League Championship of the 1967-68 season—one of the most memorable seasons in Manchester's soccer history. It was to be an incredible ding-dong struggle between City and United in the race for the championship tape. The fans were enthralled and delighted as the battle swung first one way and then the other. But the inspiring thing about this particular struggle between the two great Manchester protagonists was the friendly rivalry that the players in each camp spread to the supporters of the other club. Mike Summerbee and George Best were bosom pals. They had even moved into business together. Summerbee reveals today, 'As far as I was concerned, George was a genius. We somehow became tremendous friends, despite the rivalry between our clubs. We went into a business partnership in Manchester and I feel the fans loved our relationship. I like to think it did a lot for the feeling between the fans of both clubs. I like to think they suddenly realised you could compete with the white-hot competition of a derby, but still have a laugh and a drink afterwards. George and I were buddies and always will be. But he played in some fabulous battles between United and City and I know that neither of us would have wished for anything else but a full-blooded battle—and there were plenty of those.' They don't come better than Summerbee, either as a player or a man. He hands this accolade to Best in a relationship which is clearly a special one: 'Friendship is a precious gift and that is what George and I hold most dear.'

What really gave City the psychological edge to believe that it was going to be their title year was the titanic clash between City and United on 27 March 1968. This was the United of the killer Denis Law, the legendary Bobby Charlton, plus Irish wizard George Best, Scottish master craftsman Pat Crerand and the tiger-tackling Nobby Stiles.

'Everyone seemed to think they were going to trample on us,' recalls Allison. 'They had just nicked a win at Maine Road back in September when they licked us 2-1. We were still smarting from that. But when the lads were getting stripped in the dressing-room you could feel an air of sheer determination. Franny was cracking his usual jokes. They were ready to go out and turn it on. I could just feel it. I told them that whatever happened, even if United took the lead, they must turn up the heat and take them on in a big way.'

Allison must have seen what was coming for the enormous 63,400 crowd erupted in the very first minute when Best darted into the City box to nip the ball into the net. 'It was a sickener,' remembers Mike Doyle. 'For the first few minutes we were a bit ragged and the United fans must have reckoned it was going to be a great night for them. But we got our act together and steadily turned it round.' It was Doyle's powerful midfield play that played a major part in the comeback City made that night.

The imperturbable Colin Bell was also beginning to fire on all cylinders and it was he who drove an unstoppable shot past goalkeeper Alex Stepney. The City hordes went crazy with delight at the sight of that vivid equaliser. Now the game swung dramatically in City's favour. The blue shirts flooded forward in waves of unstoppable attacks. 'United were getting rattled,' says Mike Summerbee. 'We had the confidence and I don't think anybody had come to Old Trafford and attacked them like we did that night. We just never stopped going forward.'

Sure enough, City took the lead when versatile George Heslop forsook his defensive duties momentarily to pile into the United penalty area for a corner in the 58th minute. As the ball arched over from Tony Coleman's boot, Heslop rose perfectly to send a flashing header into the net. Bell was having an unforgettable night and when in the 64th minute he made a dangerous run into the United penalty area, defender Francis Burns brought him down for a penalty. Ice-cool Lee cracked home the spot kick and United's misery was complete.

The City fans were exultant. In only their second season back in the big time of the First Division, they had given the great United a real stuffing in their own backyard. Allison remembers, 'With a crowd as big as that and all the noise they produced, it was an absolutely unforgettable night. The City fans had a fabulous time. I think the United supporters took it well, because the ones I spoke to said we deserved that victory. It was a great sporting occasion.'

The icing was on the City cake when the dressing-room door opened not long after the final whistle and the great Matt Busby walked in with a beaming smile. 'Well done, lads,' he said as he shook Joe Mercer's hand. 'All credit to you, you deserved it.' Now City knew what they were truly capable of. 'I was already thinking about the championship,' says Malcolm. 'It was getting nearer and nearer. Joe and I were on our way to a dream.'

The season was reaching its climax which carried the sort of tension many found almost unbearable. City were neck and neck with Manchester United for the title. City's final match of the 1967-68 season was against Newcastle United at St James' Park. They had to win to have a hope of winning the title. In only their second season back in the First Division the Mercer-Allison combination was on the verge of a quite stunning success. But could they and their players keep their nerve over the last nail-biting 90 minutes that could make history?

Certainly Allison was only too well aware that they had to keep everyone relaxed. As the Manchester City team coach pulled into the huge forecourt at St James' Park the blue and white scarves of the City fans were waiting to welcome their men as they prepared for the last battle. 'It was an incredible sight,' said Allison. 'You would have thought we were the home team, there were so many blue banners and scarves on show.' Newcastle's manager Joe Harvey, the former United wing-half and skipper, told Allison when they met inside the ground, 'I think that for the first time in Newcastle United's history there are more away fans in the ground than our own supporters.'

Allison does not doubt that those fabulous City supporters played a vital role that day. 'The team were chuffed to bits to see so many fans there. It lifted them at a vital time and just gave them that little extra edge of determination to finish the job.'

The first half saw four goals scored and as Allison recalls, 'Our defenders were a bundle of nerves. I have always noticed that in tense matches it is always the men who are defending who feel the pressure more and seem to make the sort of mistakes you would never expect of them in a normal run-of-the-mill game. I suppose it is understandable, but I was horrified to see what was happening to our men in such a vital match.'

Mike Summerbee gave City an early lead only for 'Pop' Robson to equalise. Although Neil Young netted, a goal by Jack Sinclair left it poised at 2-2 at half-time. It could go either way. City's fate was in the balance. But one wild move in the shape of cutting criticism might wreck everything.

Allison was angry as he headed for the dressing-room. 'I felt I had to give them a bit of a bawling out for the way they were letting themselves down—especially those mistakes at the back,' he remembers. 'But the second I saw their faces when I opened the door, I knew that the last thing Joe and I should be doing was tearing a strip off them. You could see the tension on their faces and I knew instinctively that we simply could not panic them.' So with a prod here and there and a slap on the back, Mercer and Allison quietly worked on boosting wavering spirits, and Mercer's last words as they rose to return to the pitch were, 'Come on—go out there and show all our fans that you can still play the sort of football that we have been doing all this season—turn on the class.'

City did just that. Two more goals were plunged into the Newcastle net, the first from Young and the second from Lee. But the tension returned with a vengeance when, with five minutes still to go, Newcastle's centre-half John McNamee rose to head United's third. Those defensive nerves were showing again and the City supporters were biting their fingernails. But City held out and returned to the dressing-room to hear the news that adversaries Manchester United had lost at home to Sunderland. City had won it in style, but perfectionist Allison was still dissatisfied. 'Franny Lee scored the best goal of the match in that second half,' he insists. 'But to this day I still don't know why the referee disallowed it.'

Then, as the fans celebrated and the champagne flowed in the City dressing-room, it was revealed that Colin Bell had battled on in agony through this vital match with a nasty ankle injury. City stayed overnight at the Five Bridges Hotel at Gateshead. Early on the Sunday morning Bell was in such agony that physiotherapist Peter Blakey had to give him a massive pain-killing injection.

The triumphant City party headed back to Manchester consuming bottles of brown ale, lemonade and crisps—the real celebrations were to be in a nightclub on their return. It was before the days of the motorways and the City coach pulled up near the centre of Leeds where the players poured off the coach to spend a penny at some public toilets. The Leeds fans who were around believed that it was a coachload of City supporters until they suddenly spotted the famous faces of Mercer, Allison, Summerbee and the rest.

When the City coach finally reached the Maine Road crowd there was an enormous throng of around 5,000 fans waiting to welcome them. The sight was thrilling to the players but Mercer, nervous at having to push his way through them, stayed aboard the coach until a car was brought right to the bottom of the bus steps.

The champagne flowed as the City men went on the town celebrating in a favourite nightclub. In fact, Malcolm Allison enjoyed himself so much that when he appeared at a press conference the next morning it was revealed he had not even been to bed. 'What next for City?' he was asked. 'We will be the first team to play on the moon,' joked Allison.

CHAPTER FIVE

AT THE BEGINNING of the 1968-69 season, Manchester City were a truly formidable outfit. In three seasons they had emerged from the Second Division to take the First Division Championship in masterful style. Mercer and Allison had quickly assembled an exciting squad of players who entertained wherever they played. They had players mustard-keen for success. There were goalkeepers Harry Dowd and Ken Mulhearn, skipper Tony Book, George Heslop, Alan Oakes, Mike Doyle, Tommy Booth, Stan Bowles, Arthur Mann, Glyn Pardoe, David Connor, Tony Coleman, Bobby Owen, Colin Bell, Francis Lee, Mike Summerbee and Neil Young.

There was a tremendous spirit of camaraderie. Lee remarks, 'I cannot remember a dull day. There was always somebody pulling somebody's leg. It was not so much a team as a family. But equally, there was still this great spirit of adventure. We were kind of football "Musketeers"—all for one and one for all. Our confidence was unshakeable.'

On the Saturday before the new season got under way, City faced up to West Bromwich Albion, who had won the FA Cup the previous season, beating Everton 1-0 at Wembley, in the match for the Charity Shield. It was a massacre. City turned on the style and the power to storm to a record-breaking 6-1 victory. The goals came from Francis Lee (2), Owen (2), Neil Young and an own goal by Lovett.

Yet City made a surprisingly lethargic start to the season by their previous high standards. The biggest handicap was the absence for the first half of the season of skipper Tony Book with a nasty Achilles tendon injury. Also, City hadn't quite been able to find their killer touch of the previous season. 'We just couldn't kill teams off as we had the previous term,' said Allison. 'But the skill was still as high as ever, and so was the will to win. We just weren't getting the rub of the green either, which can play such a vital part in the push for the championship.'

It was pretty obvious to everyone at Maine Road, after a string of inconsistent results, that they were not going to retain the championship. But Malcolm still had high hopes. 'We told the lads just before Christmas that we had a definite plan,' said Allison with a grin. 'I said, now listen, you lot, you are going to win the FA Cup!'

Allison set out his plan to the players with an astonishing simple logic. 'All you have to do is win six matches and you've cracked it.' Mercer scratched his head and said, 'I never realised before that winning the FA Cup was quite as simple as that, Malcolm.'

But Malcolm's cocky crack certainly set something going in the players' minds. 'We had got into the habit of winning trophies over the past few seasons,' says Summerbee. 'The idea of getting our hands on the FA Cup became an obsession. We knew we were capable of it, mainly because of our ability to score goals—and good goals at that. There wasn't a defence that could frighten us but there were a lot of defences who were certainly scared of us.'

So a highly ambitious Manchester City rolled up their sleeves and set off on the road to Wembley. Yet, ironically, it was to be City's defence that played the major role. The first hurdle seemed easy enough—a third round tie against Third Division Luton Town at Maine Road. Yet City made hard work of it against a battling Luton side who had City's fans biting their fingernails in frustration. Eventually, it needed a second-half penalty from spot-kick ace Francis Lee to kill Luton off.

The fourth round was much tougher—an uninviting trip to St James' Park to recall memories of City's epic last match victory there which had brought them the championship in the previous season. But could they pull it off again in this tough one at Newcastle and keep their Wembley dream alive? There was also an ominous statistic concerning this tie—City had *never* beaten Newcastle in the FA Cup. But as Mercer told his men when somebody mentioned that point: 'They haven't faced *this* Manchester City side before in an FA Cup tie.'

It proved a hectic struggle. But City's defence was in rock-solid form and Newcastle had to settle for a goalless draw which meant a replay at Maine Road. Memories went flooding back to that epic FA Cup replay in 1957 between the two sides at Maine Road. In an unforgettable match, City had surged into a 3-0 lead only for Newcastle to storm back to a shock 5-4 victory after extra time. But City were not in the mood for those sort of lapses in 1969. Goals from Neil Young and Bobby Owen saw them through to the next round.

They then had a highly professional 4-1 victory over Blackburn Rovers, at Ewood Park in the next round. The tie had been postponed because of bad weather and then again because a 'flu epidemic had laid low most of the Blackburn first-team players. The game itself was a rip-roaring battle, with Lee putting City ahead and then Jim Fryatt equalising. But the unstoppable Lee scored again and Tony Coleman grabbed two more to put City into the sixth round.

The opposition on the next occasion was Tottenham Hotspur, famous for their FA Cup triumphs of the past and still a formidable outfit. Happily for City the battle was to take place at Maine Road. The game was a titanic struggle with Spurs, usually so silky-smooth, fighting like desperadoes in a fiercely competitive match. Once again, it was the never-say-die Francis Lee who proved the match winner with a great goal after 64 minutes driving the 52,000 crowd wild.

'Franny was tremendous that day,' recalls Allison. 'It was the sort of game that was always going to be won by a single goal, and he was the man of the moment. Franny always had such great stamina and he settled it with that goal. We were up in the clouds by then.'

Allison's confident battle plan—'It only takes six wins to lift the FA Cup'—was proving a very difficult philosophy to follow. But City were getting there. Their next big date was the FA Cup semi-final confrontation with Harry Catterick's Everton at Villa Park.

Once again, City found themselves battling in a nerve-tingling struggle which swung first one way and then the other. Mercer and Allison told their men at half-time, 'Stay with it! Keep your nerve! You will win it, because their defence will crack first.' With only a minute left, Villa Park suddenly exploded with thunderous roars and a sea of waving sky-blue scarves as City broke through at last. Neil Young put over a perfect corner. Up rose Mike Doyle to head the ball down to Mike Summerbee who flicked it into the path of Tommy Booth whose shot flew into the net. Mercer's men were at Wembley. City fans were delirious with delight.

Allison moved among his conquering heroes, filling the glasses with the umpteen bottles of champagne he had so confidently organised BEFORE the game. But suddenly Allison was called to the dressing-room door to see if he could comply with an extraordinary request. 'It was Everton's goalkeeper Gordon West,' says Malcolm. 'He told me their manager Harry Catterick was giving them hell in their dressing-room. He was fed up with it and wondered if he could come into our room to get away from all the hassle. So I got a glass, stuck it in his hand, and sat him down in our dressing-room. I think he must have been the only player in the losing team in an FA Cup semi-final to have joined the winners in a celebratory glass of champers. We were delighted to have him.'

Meanwhile, Mercer made a big promise as he joined in the celebrations: 'Now the tension is over, we are going to Wembley to play football.' When the big day came Mercer and Allison primed their team in the Wembley dressing-room, imploring them to keep calm and play football. So long did their instructions take that the Leicester City players, already waiting nervously in the Wembley tunnel, were out there alone for almost three minutes before Mercer's men filed out to join them for the walk on to the pitch.

There didn't seem much wrong with the nerves of City's players. Mike Summerbee cheekily asked for Princess Anne's telephone number as Her Royal Highness was introduced to the players. Tony Coleman offered his regards to Princess Anne's 'Mum and Dad'. Allison is quick to reveal that they went into this final with far too optimistic an outlook. Leicester were to prove far more difficult to overcome than he and Joe had anticipated. 'I was over-confident about it,' says Allison. 'Leicester's manager Frank O'Farrell had decided to have a real go at us and made it a very open game. He had set his stall out well. He was always a good strategist.'

City had decided against playing in their famous sky-blue shirts for this final. 'Instead, we settled for our away strip,' says Allison. 'It was because we felt it wasn't a home game and our fans always expected to see us in those colours when they saw us playing away from Maine Road. That strip was incredibly popular and at that time was the biggest selling set of shirts Umbro had had.'

Leicester's Allan Clarke, always a danger man, came desperately close to giving his side the lead with a blistering shot, but 'keeper Harry Dowd reacted like lightning to tip the ball round the post. City struck back with Neil Young driving over the top and Tony Coleman thundering one just wide of an upright. Steadily Mercer's men began to turn the screw and at last Leicester cracked under the pressure.

One great goal, superbly worked in true Manchester City style, brought them the FA Cup. The almost arrogant plan of Allison's made four months earlier to lift the trophy, became a stirring reality in the 23rd minute. Twinkle-toed Mike Summerbee set it up when he took a throw from Francis Lee and darted past Allan Woollett. In a flash he pulled back from the byline into the path of the advancing Neil Young. It couldn't have been a more perfectly timed centre and Young took his chance with a spectacular left-foot shot that flashed just under the crossbar. Leicester's England Under-23 goalkeeper, Peter Shilton, destined to make so many unbelievable saves in a glittering full England career, could do nothing about it.

That was the winner. Mercer and Allison had pulled off yet another amazing triumph. It seemed a never-ending dream. For so long City's magnificent supporters had had to shuffle disconsolately in the shadows as those Manchester United fans danced a jig on the sunny side of the street. Now City were wallowing in their success as it flowed on and on.

There was a wonderful surprise for Tony Coleman following his jocular Wembley remark to Princess Anne, asking her to give his best regards to her parents. One or two people in the City camp felt that Coleman might have been over-familiar with Royalty and that his remark hadn't been well received. They could not have been more wrong—the letter bearing the stamp of Buckingham Palace and addressed to Coleman arrived at Maine Road shortly after City's Cup final triumph. Coleman opened it in amazement and read that it was a message from an equerry, saying Her Majesty the Queen had asked her to write and thank him on behalf of herself and the Duke of Edinburgh for his kind remarks to them, passed on by their daughter.

CHAPTER SIX

MANCHESTER DERBIES crackle like tinderwood and flare and dazzle the eye of the beholder. There is never an empty seat, yet it is rarely that the fans even manage to sit on them. They are almost always on their feet, swept up in the emotion of the battle. That's the way it is when Red meets Blue and the excitement reaches fever pitch after a week of fierce argument at work or in the pubs as to who will triumph in the end. There is a high, almost unbearable, antici-pation of the struggle to come.

So when City and United reached the semi-final of the League Cup in the December of 1969, Manchester's soccer followers pun-ched the air in delight. This was it, each side declared. This was the showdown they had all been waiting for. The diplomatic Matt Busby welcomed the clash, but he added with a wry smile, 'It will be a tough game and could be very, very close.' Typically, Matt got it dead right.

Malcolm Allison, as ever, revelled in the nerve-testing build-up to these two crunch clashes between the old antagonists. His confidence was unshakeable as always—and so was Joe Mercer's. Mercer told me in an interview shortly after the draw revealed City and United faced one another that he welcomed the massive collision between the two great clubs that would leave one the triumphant and exultant victor, with the loser smarting in the pain of defeat. 'We have shown not only that we are capable of winning major trophies,' said Joe, 'but that we can win them with style. We're a little cocky, if you like. But, after all, that's not a bad thing, is it? Especially here in Manchester, after all the years that City fans have seen United holding court. But it is different now. It's going to be a great semi-final, and, as it is over two legs, whoever wins will surely be able to say they were the complete masters—not as if it were a 90-minute ding-dong job. It is a real contest and I feel confident that our lads are going to prove that they are the best in the business now . . . And what could be better than beating United?' he added, with a twinkle in his eye.

Joe could well afford to show this confidence for the old foe. Less than a month earlier, his team had crushed United 4-0 at Maine Road in their League match in front of 63,013 exultant fans. It was City at their most dominant in the derby for longer than anyone could remember. They had stamped their class right across a game that saw Busby's highly rated United eleven leaving the pitch with faces as scarlet as their famous shirts.

Allison was in a night club, enjoying a relaxing glass of champagne three days before the first leg. I asked him how he thought the game would go. 'Well, to be honest, after what we did to them in the League game at Maine Road, I'll be surprised if they turn up,' he grinned, knocking the ash off the end of his cigar. But Allison's fun and ability to take the tension out of these big confrontations could not disguise the fact that he knew more than anybody that this was a historical milestone for the great City club. They had won the League Championship and the FA Cup in a swashbuckling style that had set the supporters of attacking football everywhere drooling in their after-match drinks. But now it was a nerve-tingling moment. What if they were to lose their nerve, falter in that flow of confidence? What could be worse if this extraordinary charge of the City bandwagon in search of further rich success should be brought to a shuddering standstill by none other than their arch-rivals across the road—Manchester United? 'For most of us, it didn't bear thinking about,' said Glyn Pardoe.

Well, if some of City's mighty band of supporters had a few qualms and headed to their local for a couple of drinks to boost their flagging confidence for the battle to come, Allison was in unshakeable mood. 'We have done so much since Joe and I came here—and so quickly—that a challenge like this is the best possible thing that can happen. United? What better opposition could we have? We have just beaten them 4-0 in the League match, so they aren't actually going to be rubbing their hands over meeting us in this one, are they?'

The League clash between the arch rivals had taken place on 15 November at Maine Road. For United fans it was a humbling experience. Colin Bell, who was making an indelible mark on English football, scored twice, Neil Young got another and an own goal by David Sadler completed City's rip-roaring triumph. 'That was something for the supporters,' recalls Allison. 'The team had real confidence now. But they also had terrific staying power. The plan to build up their stamina and strength was really paying off. They were going as hard in the last two minutes of a game as they had been in the first two. Remember how many top players United had at that time, like Denis Law, George Best, Bobby Charlton and Pat Crerand. They were full of world stars yet we still walloped them. That was why we went into the two semi-final legs of the League Cup with so much confidence. We had reached a point where we felt we were capable of anything as long as everyone played to their full potential.'

It was ironic that United should now be poised, along with City, to enjoy the rich pickings from the huge gates that the semi-final was to bring at their respective grounds. At the trophy's inception in 1960 United had been among the many top clubs to spurn the tournament. They believed it would never really take off like the FA Cup and would not be a money-spinner.

Mike Summerbee, who was playing such a vital role in Mercer's army of magnificence as it thundered ever forwards, recalled this moment of vivid confrontation. 'It was the duel the fans wanted and the players were just as delighted,' he told me. 'It was ironic that I should be facing a team in the semi-final of the League Cup for whom played George Best, my best pal. But when the draw was known, we chatted to one another immediately, as we always did, and pulled one another's legs. It was electric. George said to me, "Isn't it great to be part of it all, no matter what turns out in the end?" That was how we felt. It was a truly great moment in Manchester's soccer history.'

There was incredible tension as the teams marched out for the first leg of the semi-final tie at Maine Road. It might have been bitingly cold but the cauldron of excitement had the 55,799 fans breathless with anticipation.

Allison's rock-solid confidence before the crunch game seemed well borne out when the powerful-moving Bell cruised through the United defence to put City ahead after 13 minutes. City fans were exultant—surely this was going to be their night. But United were certainly not in the mood to cave in as they had in that 4-0 League defeat at Maine Road earlier. Best produced a flash of his special magic with a cunning centre that Brian Kidd met to send a header zipping just inches past the post.

From the start of the second half the old Red defiance was clear in United's change of style. It was all-out attack from those famous red shirts and the United fans threw their vocal support behind their idols. The magnificent Charlton started to test City's defence with those long, surging runs down the flanks and jinking Best started to dazzle as only he can. Sure enough, it was Best who set up the chance that Charlton doesn't miss and United were level. But City rallied after surviving a further storm of United attacks to come up with the winner. Lee went on one of his famous charges down the middle. In a desperate attempt to halt his progress, Ian Ure brought him down in the penalty area. Referee Jack Taylor pointed to the spot and City's fans held their breath as Lee himself placed the ball and walked back to take the kick. Goalkeeper Alex Stepney just felt the swish of the ball as it blasted past him in typical Lee style. City had won the first leg 2-1. But would it be enough for the second encounter at Old Trafford?

The epic struggle in that second leg at Old Trafford had the 63,000 fans in a state of constant fervour. It was one of the finest battles between the two clubs ever fought. It seemed to swing first United's way, then City's.

A great blow to City's hopes for the second leg came with a shock injury to their danger man, Colin Bell. Bell had played for England against Portugal at Wembley on the week before the United match. He was brought down in the second half and clutched his shoulder in agony. The trouble was diagnosed as torn shoulder ligaments and that ruled him out of the big Old Trafford clash. It was a sad blow and United fans were strutting the streets promising City supporters that without the smooth-flowing Bell their chances of surviving at Old Trafford were gone.

United caused a surprise by including the great Denis Law for the second leg, despite the fact that the dazzling Scottish ace wasn't really at peak fitness. It was a freezing December evening and Old Trafford was bulging at the seams.

In the City dressing-room, Mercer and Allison moved among their men, cracking jokes—anything to ease the nervousness that inevitably gets to the players on these big occasions. Says Allison:

'Francis Lee was always a great one to have in your dressing-room on those big match occasions. He was remarkable. Nothing seemed to bother him. He was nerveless, even as a young player. He loved the challenge.' But you could feel the tension in the air as the red and then the sky-blue shirts appeared on the Old Trafford pitch for battle. They were now one match from Wembley.

It was City who stormed into the lead early in the first half with a goal that set their fans roaring with delight. Neil Young tried a powerful low drive that goalkeeper Alex Stepney did well to block. The rebound ran to Lee who whacked it back in, only for Ian Ure to stick a foot out. The ball flew to young Ian Bowyer who hammered an unstoppable drive past the helpless Stepney.

But there are no more dangerous opponents than Manchester United when they are behind—and especially at Old Trafford. Before half-time, they were level. It was that master midfield craftsman Paddy Crerand who created the opening with a superb through ball into the path of United player Paul Edwards. The youngster rose to the occasion by producing a stunning, rising drive that flashed just under the bar with 'keeper Joe Corrigan having not the slightest chance. Now it was the huge army of United supporters who were in full voice, urging their men to finish City off.

'It was a tremendous match,' Mike Summerbee recalls. 'It just kept swaying this way and that, but we never lost our confidence. We kept calling to one another that we could do it. It was vital that we believed in ourselves under that sort of pressure.'

But when George Best set off on one of his mesmerising runs, the City fans held their breath. The Irish wizard whipped in a low shot that goalkeeper Joe Corrigan did well to block. Denis Law pounced on the rebound like a hawk on a mouse and United led on the night 2-1. It was now 2-2 on aggregate.

With only two minutes to go City won an indirect free kick on the edge of the penalty area. Up stepped Lee to blast the ball over the United wall and a little to the right of goalkeeper Alex Stepney. With an instinctive reaction Stepney parried the ball away, but in darted Mike Summerbee to drive the ball past the helpless 'keeper for a goal that levelled the game 2-2 on the night and gave City a vital 4-3 victory on aggregate. Stepney claimed afterwards that he believed the kick was a DIRECT one. But the video of that match showed referee Jim Finney holding his left arm raised high as Lee started to run towards the ball for his shot.

So City were once again at Wembley with the chance of completing a clean sweep of the trophies over three seasons with the Championship and the FA Cup already won. 'We really enjoy going to Wembley,' grinned Allison. 'It is becoming like a second home to us.' But Joe Mercer was wary of their opponents, West Bromwich Albion. 'They are a very good side and we are going to have to be at our best if we are to win. This will be some match—it is going to be exciting.' In those thrilling days of Mercer and Allison, it always was . . .

CHAPTER SEVEN

IRONICALLY, CITY were drawn to face another trip to Old Trafford in the fourth round of the FA Cup. Here was the chance for revenge for Matt Busby's men for that bitter League Cup semi-final defeat by City. And, for once, Mercer's men failed to find that vital spark of inspiration against their old rivals. United dominated the match completely, running out comfortable 3-0 winners. 'We never got into the game,' says Allison. 'It was one of those instances when the team never played anywhere near its true potential.'

In fact, as City approached the League Cup final with West Brom, the team were looking exceedingly jaded. That zip and sparkle which was such a hallmark of their normal game seemed to mysteriously disappear. They had won only a couple of League matches in three months. Injuries hadn't helped their situation but there was a real loss of form. Neil Young, in particular, was nothing like the same player who had proved such a goal plunderer in the previous season when he had grabbed a great winner to land City the FA Cup. Unhappily, Mercer and Allison had decided to drop him.

City fans fretted over the lack of vigour in their normally rampant team. Yet could they rekindle the spark and still set Wembley on fire on the big day? The big occasion always seemed to bring out the scintillating best in the Mercer-Allison sides and, sure enough, Wembley brought them back to life.

Only three days earlier they had been fighting out a goalless draw against Coimbra in Portugal, in the first leg of the third round of the European Cup Winners' Cup–hardly the ideal preparation for the

West Brom final. On the day itself the Wembley pitch was a mud heap in comparison to the green velvet carpet players and spectators alike had come to expect. Joe Mercer was horrified. This wasn't the sort of surface his silk-smooth passers of the ball could play their magnificent football on. 'It's a pig of a pitch,' snorted Joe. 'I have never seen Wembley like this. But we will just have to get on with it.'

If City needed inspiration on this day, then they found it in the figure of Francis Lee. He was to prove a mercurial worker and fighter in the thick of the battle. He was a man inspired and Allison explains why. 'Franny couldn't get going in the FA Cup final against Leicester. Although we had won, he felt disappointed at his contribution. He sets himself very high standards and was determined to make up for it in the League Cup final. Once out there, he just roared at the lads, "Give it to me, I'll win this one for you." He was phenomenal out there.'

Yet the final started disastrously for City. As early as the sixth minute Albion took the lead to send their supporters wild, leaving City's fans with sinking feelings in their stomachs. Albion's aggressive England striker Jeff Astle harassed Tony Book, who conceded a corner. This was half-cleared and Ray Wilson put the ball back into the City penalty area. Up rose Astle to head powerfully past goalkeeper Joe Corrigan with City's defence in complete disarray. A goal down so early wasn't the best thing for morale and Mercer and Allison watched anxiously from their seats to see how their men would react to this shock setback.

But from that moment on City took command with Lee storming here, there and everywhere as he boosted the confidence of the fighting blues. Allison recalls, 'I had said to Joe, "That will wake them up and make them play now. They were hurt by that goal."' Allison was right. City steadily took command. The determined Mike Doyle and the thrusting Alan Oakes carried the battle deep into Albion's half with a series of adventurous raids. This was City pushing forward, turning on the style as only they could at this period of their development. It was attack, attack, attack. Yet Albion almost caught them out on the break as City pushed forward a little too far in search of an equaliser. Suggett was put through, completely clear down the middle. Had he assessed the situation more carefully and taken his time, he might have scored. But as happens so often in a big game, the tension played its part and he shot wildly wide. He revealed afterwards that he had believed he was offside anyway. Yet he wasn't. But that wise old sage Mercer said philosophically afterwards, 'That was close, but that's a cup final for you. You have to take your chances. From that moment on we got on top of the job.'

Sure enough, in the 60th minute City broke through at last and the roars of acclamation for the goal came thundering from the huge army of their supporters packed into the Wembley arena. A corner by Pardoe was flicked on by Summerbee. Bell headed a beautiful pass into the path of Mike Doyle who made no mistake with a fierce drive that rocketed into the back of the Albion net.

But then City were struck a real blow when the brilliant Summerbee limped off with a leg injury. Off he went to hospital where an X-ray revealed he had a hairline fracture of the left leg. 'It was tough having to come off like that just at a point with the game in the balance,' says Mike. 'But I still felt our lads had a grip of the game and that they weren't going to let go of it.' It was double agony for Mike because he could not wait and watch the finish of the game but had to speed by ambulance to hospital. Ian Bowyer took his place whilst Albion's Asa Hartford, who ironically was to become a big City favourite later in his career, was substituted for Dick Kryzwicki. But at the end of the 90 minutes, the match was still locked in a 1-1 draw.

So the final moved into extra time and Allison recalls, 'Joe and I were confident we had the greater physical reserves needed to win the game. We told the lads that they had to take the game to West Brom. The order was attack and they obeyed it brilliantly.' That was well illustrated by the fact that normal defender Glyn Pardoe who, along with Lee and Doyle, had a dazzling afternoon, grabbed the winning goal in extra time. He raced up to squeeze the ball home between goalkeeper John Osborne and the far post to send the City masses wild. So skipper Tony Book went up to the Royal Box once again and this time held aloft the League Cup for the breathless City supporters to hail their heroes.

It had been a great victory. After that disappointing run since their tremendous two-leg semi-final over United back in December, the City supporters had worried in case their team might have lost that magical winning knack. They had their answer at Wembley. Now, in four quite unbelievable years, Mercer and Allison had lifted them from the depths of the Second Division to the heady heights of sensational soccer glory. They won the Second Division Champion-ship, the League Championship, the FA Cup and now the League Cup. 'Not a bad little haul,' grinned Mercer, happily drinking champagne with a beaming Allison at his side.

But there was still another piece of silverware to be won, and this time it was in Europe. For City's next big date was the final of the European Cup Winners Cup against Gornik Zabrze in the huge Prater Stadium in Vienna. This was City's second venture into Europe after Malcolm's first bold prediction—'We'll terrify Europe!'—had come badly unstuck the previous season when City had gone out of the European Cup in the first round to the little-known Turkish side, Fenerbache. But their impressionable drive for the European Cup Winners Cup had both style and piratical flourish about it. This was the City team who could take on anyone with confidence and a flash of defiance, even if the ball didn't break their way.

It certainly didn't in their first round match against the highly rated Spanish side Atletico Bilbao. It was ironic that Atletico was managed by Ronnie Allen, the former West Brom player, who was impressing the Spanish and European soccer scene with his style. The first leg was fought out in the San Mames stadium and City found themselves two goals down after only 11 minutes. But now they were to show the real spirit of the Mercer-Allison alliance which had been deeply forged in the side. They had been told that if the going got tough then they had to strike back even harder. City's snarling retaliation was vicious. Allison recalls with pride, 'They battled and they fought every inch of the way. The Spaniards were amazed at their resilience. They had expected our lads would just cave in and call it a day. I only wish that every City supporter could have been in that stadium on that day. They would have been so proud and would have been able to carry the memory of the team's great fight back in their minds forever.' City battled back for a magnificent 3-3 draw, thanks to strikes by Neil Young and Tommy Booth plus an own goal by Echeverria.

So City went into the second leg at Maine Road with their tails up. Atletico were never given a chance. City whipped them 3-0 with Ian Bowyer, Colin Bell and Alan Oakes grabbing the goals. Now it looked as if Allison's proud boast wasn't going to be so wide of the mark after all.

In the second round City had an easy time against Belgian club Lierse SK. In the first leg in Belgium they won 3-0 thanks to two goals from Francis Lee and one from Colin Bell. The second leg at Maine Road was a 5-0 cakewalk with goals from Bell (2), Lee (2) and Mike Summerbee. Then in the quarter final they met the Students of Academica, of Portugal. City were well organised for a goalless draw in the first leg in Portugal, but the second leg at Maine Road was a fierce battle with the Portuguese showing hostile tactics that angered both the City camp and their supporters. City just pulled it off thanks to an extra time goal from Tony Towers who had come on as a substitute for George Heslop.

In the semi-final, City faced the crack German outfit Schalke 04 who were renowned as knock-out specialists. It was ironic that Allison was at this time banned from touchline coaching because of punishment handed out in England. Nonetheless, Joe Mercer and his coach had their players in tip-top shape for the coming tussle.

I have conducted many long interviews with the City players of that time and there is no doubt the Mercer-Allison chemistry worked wonders. It is that indefinable something that produces a formula for success that you get in all walks of life. It is an understanding, a belief in ability that projects players to perform almost beyond their wildest dreams. And when they watch their performances on videos years later, they exclaim, 'Was that really me?'

Well, City faced up to the Germans with a cool determination after an expert briefing by Mercer and Allison, who had decided upon their tactics for the coming struggle. The Germans won the first leg on their own ground 1-0. But City were more than satisfied with the result. 'We knew we had the strength and the class to win the second leg at Maine Road,' said Malcolm. 'The lads did a great job.'

Excitement in Manchester was at fever pitch for the second leg. But the players were cool. Says Francis Lee, 'There was a confidence in the side now that was quite remarkable. We just believed in our all-round ability to be capable of beating anyone—and after all, we had already proved it.' That summing up was exactly right. City fans were in celebratory mood from the start as their heroes tore the Germans apart. They raced into a 3-0 lead by half-time and that was the end of the match. The Germans pretty well capitulated, leaving City 5-2 winners and finalists to await the victors of the match between Gornik and Roma who were locked in a long, drawn-out struggle in the other semi-final. City's marksmen were Neil Young

(2), Colin Bell, Francis Lee and Mike Doyle. After two drawn matches, Gornik finally won through and City knew at last the team they had to beat if they were to win a big European trophy to go with the stunning display of local silverware they had picked up in their extraordinary rise to the pinnacle of football in this country.

So City flew into Vienna to meet Gornik in the Prater stadium for a European shoot-out. The Maine Road hot-shots showed what they were made of by storming into a 2-0 half-time lead in a match played under a torrential cloudburst more usually accepted as the infamous Manchester weather. It was the rejuvenated Neil Young, restored to the side after a period of being left out of the first team picture, who grabbed the first goal in only 12 minutes. It was Lee who created the goal with a thrusting charge in the Polish penalty area before releasing a shot of fingertip-burning power that caused the goalkeeper to parry the ball. In a flash, Neil Young was on the rebound to plunge the ball into the net. Then two minutes from half-time City won a penalty when the uncontrollable Young surged into the penalty area. Polish goalkeeper Kostka, faced with a one-to-one situation, decided his only hope was to bring down Young, and he did. Austrian referee Paul Schiller immediately pointed to the penalty spot and up stepped Lee to hammer the ball home. The rain poured down but City were singing. Despite the Gornik's skipper Oslizlo pulling one back in the 68th minute, there was never a danger of City surrendering their grip on the game.

Once again Manchester City had pulled it off. It seemed that there was nothing they couldn't accomplish. It was a time of deep satisfaction. Says the tough-tackling Mike Doyle, who was the epitome of City's never-say-die spirit: 'At that time we felt there was nothing we could not achieve. Despite all the trophies we had won, we were certain there were going to be many more to follow. There was no feeling of lethargy. We loved being up there at the top. It was a fabulous time.'

Malcolm Allison pays special tribute to the contribution during those glory days to pencil-slim winger Neil Young. The skilful Young had that extraordinary ability to produce thunderous left-foot shots which brought City so many wonderful goals. Young had been around quite a bit before the great Mercer-Allison union arrived at Maine Road. He had even been born close to the City ground. He was a regular Blues fan and, in his youth, could be found on the Maine Road terraces most Saturdays. He made his début when he was only 17 against Aston Villa in the 1961-62 season—surprisingly, playing on the right wing. He made a big impact alongside the likes of Peter Dobing and Joe Hayes and quickly showed an exciting knack of finding the net in his first season at senior level. He scored ten League goals in his 24 games of that first season in the senior side. But once Joe and Malcolm arrived to drive City back into the First Division Young really blossomed. He had already played under two managers at City before Mercer came—dour Scot Les McDowall and George Poyser—but it was under the guidance of Mercer and Allison that Young really took off. The highlight of Young's career was his dynamic strike for the winning goal in the 1-0 victory over Leicester City in the 1968-69 FA Cup final. 'Neil had a superb balance and pace,' says Allison. 'He was a better player than he realised. He had so much talent. Sometimes I felt that his confidence wasn't quite as strong as it should have been. But when he was on form there was no better winger to watch when he went for goal.'

CHAPTER EIGHT

A CROP of injuries during the 1970-71 season cruelly handicapped City's chances of winning any trophies in that spell. But it did see the emergence of an exciting group of young players who stepped boldly into the breach and proved the Blues had a great scouting system. One exciting newcomer in the ranks was Freddie Hill from Third Division Halifax Town. Once again, Mercer and Allison had gone into the lower divisions for a veteran player—midfielder Hill was 31. It brought back memories of that famous signing of Tony Book who was also in his late playing years when City signed him. For Hill it was a golden chance to sample soccer at the top when he must have thought opportunity had passed him by six years previously. That was when he was about to sign for the great Liverpool, managed by Bill Shankly. Yet the transfer fell through because the unfortunate Hill was found to have high blood pressure. Hill said of that medical when he signed for City, 'It was all down to over-excitement. I was heartbroken when the move fell through. I couldn't believe there was anything wrong with me. There wasn't, in fact. I saw a specialist who confirmed there was no problem. I was just worked up by all the excitement.' So Hill eventually ended up with Halifax. 'When I heard Manchester City had come in for me it just didn't seem possible,' he said.

Could his old Bolton buddy Francis Lee have played a part in this sudden swoop for Hill? I reckon Lee must have urged Malcolm Allison to snap up schemer Hill. The price of £12,000 was cheap for a player with two England caps and who had made 12 appearances in the England Under-23 side.

City made a rampant start to the new season, winning six and drawing two of their first eight games before losing 2-0 at Tottenham Hotspur. But injuries around the middle of the season to players like Mike Summerbee, Alan Oakes, Glyn Pardoe, George Heslop and goalkeeper Joe Corrigan and others meant it was time to blood some of the younger players. Goalkeeper Ron Healey, Willie Donachie, Ian Mellor, Frank Garrodus, Derek Jeffries, Ian Bowyer all came into the side, impressed and showed the breadth of talent in the squad. Although the disruption caused by the injuries meant City were just not strong enough for a title charge there was one memorable League match that season for the Blues. It was 12 December at Old Trafford when City ripped Manchester United's defence apart for a 4-1 victory. There was a riveting hat-trick from Francis Lee with another goal provided by a gleeful Doyle, a man always so delighted to lick United.

But it was in Europe where City excelled, considering their weakened resources. The young bloods did City proud and there were some memorable moments as they battled through round after round of the European Cup Winners Cup that season. Ironically, the first hurdle was a round one confrontation with Irish League side Linfield which they would have been expected to clear comfortably. After a 1-0 home win in the first leg thanks to a Colin Bell strike, they lost 2-1 at Linfield in the second leg but scraped through on the away goals rule thanks to Francis Lee's strike. The second round, in October, brought City up against the crack Hungarian side Honved. Yet City sailed past them. A Francis Lee goal gave City a 1-0 away victory in the first leg. Back at Maine Road, City won 2-0 thanks to goals from Colin Bell and Francis Lee for a 3-0 victory on aggregate to set up a memorable clash with Gornik Zabrze of Poland. When City went down 2-0 in the away first leg of the third round it was clear they were going to be up against it in the return game at Maine Road, but with a crowd of 31,950 roaring them on the Blues pulled it back by winning 2-0 with goals from Ian Mellor and Mike Doyle. So that meant a replay in Copenhagen. City rose magnificently to their task. 'We really turned it on,' recalls Francis Lee. 'We were told to go out and attack and we roasted them.' Goals from Tommy Booth, Lee and Neil Young gave City a comfortable 3-1 victory. But in the semi-final

Chelsea were to prove too tough for them. They lost 1-0 at Stamford Bridge in the first leg in April and although a crowd of 43,663 at Maine Road gave them massive support the Blues went down 0-1 to give Chelsea an aggregate win of 2-0. It had been a brave season by a City team forced to bring in youngsters who had done them proud in a stiff season against top opposition.

City plunged into the transfer market for a new forward on 2 August before the start of the 1971-72 season as they prepared to make another drive for the League Championship. The man they plumped for was a big surprise to most of the City fans. He was the tall Welsh international Wyn Davies, then with Newcastle United. Davies was the ideal man as far as Francis Lee was concerned—they had played together at Bolton Wanderers before Lee joined City. The lanky Davies had a formidable reputation for his heading ability. But the reason for a lot of eyebrows being raised when City paid £60,000 for him was that in his recent First Division games for Newcastle he had scored only two goals. Allison explains, 'Joe and I felt that we needed a big man in the middle to knock balls down for Franny and the others to feed on. Wyn was terrific at doing that.' Certainly, Lee was delighted with the arrival of the big Welshman. 'He gave us a lot of extra power up front and he was as brave as a lion,' he says. 'He was a far better player than a lot of onlookers realised. He was wonderful for me by the way he knocked the ball into my path.'

It certainly did pay off for expert striker Lee—he was to rattle in 33 League and Cup goals in that first season Davies joined up with him. Ironically, City would so easily have landed Davies five years earlier when he moved from Bolton to Newcastle United. Mercer and Allison had already been alerted to the heading power of Davies and along with several other top clubs they were ready to compete with Newcastle. The Geordies pipped everybody to pull the Davies' signature. Yet Davies said at the time that he would have been happy to join City as he wasn't really keen about leaving Lancashire where he had finally settled down after joining Bolton from Wrexham. 'It was only after I had joined Newcastle that I read of City's interest in the newspapers,' said Davies. He had a special warmth for City boss Mercer as Joe had made a big impression on him when Davies had trials for Aston Villa at the time Mercer was the manager there. Another big irony was that Davies could quite easily have started his career across the road at Old Trafford, for he was also given trials by Manchester United. But he decided not to pursue his chances with the Reds. Davies felt they had too many forwards on their staff already.

Mercer and Allison were rubbing their hands with glee at the way things were working out in that early part of the season. 'Wyn was perfect for Mike Summerbee's centres,' Allison says. 'The rest of the lads loved having him up there and doing such a great job laying the ball off for them. He was very, very brave, and with Franny coming in behind and picking up the goals match after match it all started to work like a well-oiled machine. The goals flowed from Franny and Davies snapped up a few himself.'

Manchester City were the fun club to visit during this breathtaking string of victories under Joe Mercer and Malcolm Allison. The Maine Road set-up had an aura of sheer pleasure and happiness about the place. Anyone who stepped into the club felt immediately welcome. Everyone was enthusiastic and, most of all, there was an air of confidence. Joe and Malcolm had done a hell of a lot—but surely there was more to come? Certainly Joe and Malcolm set out into the fresh season of 1971-72 with renewed determination to win the League Championship again. More than the Division One title itself, they saw it as the door that would open for them to have a crack at the European Cup—the Holy Grail of all great football clubs. It would be the final accolade to their remarkable partnership and the reward to their loyal supporters. There were springs in the steps of these City men. Mercer had told them, 'Turn on the style now. Give the fans something they really enjoy—win with confidence.'

Francis Lee was in phenomenal scoring form, rattling in goal after goal. Yet the season did not go well. There were early Cup exits. They went out of the FA Cup in a third round replay at Middlesbrough, who beat them 1-0 at Ayresome Park after a 1-1 draw at Maine Road. City beat Wolves 4-3 in the League Cup but lost 3-0 to Bolton Wanderers at Burnden Park in the second round—ironically, to a hat-trick from Manchester-born Gary Jones.

So the championship was their only hope. It seemed within their capabilities as the season progressed, with City jockeying for a position at the top along with Derby County, Leeds United and Liverpool. But well though City were going, Allison felt they could still use a player with extra flair—someone who would not only give

Francis Lee in spectacular action against Spurs at White Hart Lane in 1970. Spurs won 2–0

Wing wizard Mike Summerbee takes on West Ham defender Billy Bonds in a match at Maine Road in 1968. Bonds is now manager of the Hammers

Big pals George Best and Mike Summerbee with Mike's bride Tina after their marriage in 1968 when George was best man

Typical Francis Lee . . . the City striker shows his defiance during the match against Crystal Palace in 1972 when City won 2–1

City's dazzling trio together in 1972. From the left Rodney Marsh, Francis Lee and Mike Summerbee having a look around Summerbee's famous shirt shop in Manchester

*City's majestic Colin Bell in action. His brilliance has made people
compare him with the legendary Peter Doherty, another Maine Road idol*

City's great manager Joe Mercer toasts Manchester United's striker Mark Hughes after presenting him with the award of Young Footballer of the Month in 1984

Former City manager Ron Saunders who went to Aston Villa and proved a masterful manager, winning the First Division Championship for them

Malcolm Allison, City's dashing coach and later manager, pictured with Tony Book, former classy skipper and later manager of the club. But their partnership on Allison's return to Maine Road was doomed to failure

Former City chairman Peter Swales pictured last year. During his 20 years in power at Maine Road, City won only one League Cup

The flamboyant John Bond acknowledges the cheers of the City supporters at Maine Road when he took over as manager in 1980

Billy McNeill, the great former Celtic player and manager, pictured at Maine Road in May 1985 after taking over as City's new team boss

Howard Kendall pictured here during his days as City manager

Peter Reid, pictured during his Everton playing days. He took over as player-manager when Howard Kendall quit as Maine Road boss and returned to his old love, Everton

the team more bite, but also a player who would give the fans some extra entertainment.

I have no doubt that Allison was a little jealous of United's star performer, the enigmatic George Best, who had people cheering in disbelief at some of his quite astonishing antics with a ball. He could hoodwink anybody and there were capacity crowds whenever he appeared. He had megastar quality. Allison told Mercer one day that he reckoned they should have a superstar of their own. Why not buy colourful Rodney Marsh from Queens Park Rangers? Marsh, Allison argued, like Best, was an enormous crowd puller and crowd pleaser. He would be money on the gate. Mercer was a little sceptical. He felt that the team was on song for the championship. Maybe they could win it without the skills and thrills of Marsh. Nevertheless, Marsh would be another jewel to add to the City crown and a glittering one at that. Maybe his sort of charisma would help cast a spell and swing the title their way. After further deliberations with Malcolm, Mercer agreed they should pay Queens Park Rangers £200,000 in March 1972. So Marsh arrived. Everyone argued over his signing. Now, would it work out?

There were nine matches to go for the championship. If City finished with anything like a winning flourish then the title would be back at Maine Road. Mercer and Allison rubbed their hands in anticipation. Yet already within the City camp itself many of the players felt a little uneasy at the newcomer in their midst. That he had exceptional ability was not in question, they all agreed. But was the Marsh style going to gel with City's style? Wasn't there a danger that Marsh might need a little time to settle in before he proved effective? If that was to be the case, then there were danger signals—time was one thing City did *not* have. They had to perform at least very near to the peak over the last nine matches in the sprint to the championship tape. If Marsh caused a slip-up, then all was lost.

The sceptics claim they were proved chillingly right. Marsh did need time to settle into the City style. City's bid for the title collapsed in a bitterly disappointing final run which brought only ten points from those final nine fixtures. They missed the championship by one point and Derby County took the title. It was a bitter pill to swallow. Today many of the City aces in that race for the title maintain that it was the decision to bring in Marsh—great player though he undoubtedly was—at that critical moment that cost them dearly. They are convinced his signing cost them the championship.

Yet it must be remembered that Marsh scored a great goal and contributed magnificently in City's 3-1 defeat of old enemies United at Old Trafford in the conclusion to the season.

Allison is philosophical about the decision to buy Marsh and plunge him straight into the thick of things with the title so precariously balanced. And he is typically honest in his reappraisal of his decision. With hindsight he says, 'I didn't realise he wasn't anywhere near the physical fitness required to join in that last push. He wasn't up to the high standard of fitness that City had reached. I'd forgotten the exceptional peak of physical experience our team had reached. That was what let him down a little, I'm afraid. At one point I acknowledged it, dropped him for a game and brought in Tony Towers in his place.'

Skipper Tony Book remembers bitterly how close they were to a second title and the chance of a tilt at the European Cup which would have gone with it. 'Rodney was a great player but when Malcolm brought him in we realised he wasn't quite fit enough for the powerful squad we had then. It wasn't his fault at all. He gave it all he had and played some good stuff. But the point was that it upset the balance—especially the attacking balance—of the team. It all went haywire and we lost our momentum and our confidence a little. I feel if the team had been left alone at this point, we would have taken the championship. Maybe Rodney could have been brought in next season when the time was right and things would have been a lot better. It was heartbreaking to see it all go up in smoke. But that's the game of football. You can come so close and yet so far . . .'

City's teak-tough defender Glyn Pardoe, who played such a splendid role during these great Mercer-Allison years of success, agrees that the decision to bring in Marsh cost them dearly. 'But let's say immediately, it wasn't Rod's fault. He was a player of real class. It was simply that there was no need to bring in any new player. We all felt we were going to win the title. Our tails were up. There was that old City confidence. Joe was bubbling and everything seemed to be going for us. But Malcolm felt that Rod would be the icing on the cake. He was confident that by bringing in Rodney it would give us an even greater chance of winning. But it didn't. Rodney tried his damnedest. But, for a start, he wasn't anywhere near our physical fitness. Again it wasn't his fault. But also it was difficult for a player of his exceptional style to come straight in and click right away. He would go off on one of his runs and the rest of the lads couldn't know exactly where the move was going. They couldn't relate. It takes time for a player of his class—and it was great class—to fit in. We lost our rhythm and suddenly the championship had slipped away.'

Roy Bailey, assistant to physiotherapist Freddie Griffiths at that time, recalls Marsh's arrival. 'It was pretty obvious to all of us that he wasn't near the high standard of physical fitness that we had at Maine Road,' says Bailey. 'The squad used to be put through some gruelling sessions that went on and on with no let up. It was the way the players had to build up their stamina. I remember when the lads were going through the drill up at a local park, seeing Rod physically sick at the side of a wall. It would have happened to any new player coming to City at that time. The players had to go through sheer hell. But they were incredibly fit at the end of it. It was the big reason for City winning so many big games at the very last gasp. They could stay the pace better than anyone.' Roy took over as physio at City during the '80s, playing a key role.

Mike Summerbee agrees. 'Rodney Marsh had a fabulous ability and there are very few more exciting players to watch. But it was Malcolm's decision to bring him in at that last tense moment, just when we were poised for the championship. It was a big mistake because you couldn't expect a new man to come in and just hit it off as if he'd been in the team for years. We had a particular pattern. Everyone had a role to play. Everyone knew the other's little bit of style. You knew instinctively what you had to do, where another man would be, when he would let it go, and the whole pattern of our play had been well balanced. Rodney came in and we lost our poise. Hard though he tried, he just couldn't quite bring it off. He had a real go and scored some wonderful goals. But it upset the apple-cart in the end and we lost a title we should have won.'

Summerbee was as sad as anyone when Mercer and Allison split in the close season. 'I believe that if they had stayed together for another couple of seasons we could have done so much more. Joe was the perfect man at the top whilst Malcolm was superb as a coach. The two complemented one another. But you had to have the leadership of Mercer. If they had kept up that relationship, I believe there would have been even more achieved.'

CHAPTER NINE

MANY PLAYERS had been well aware of the struggle for power within the boardroom that was to lead to the elevation of Malcolm Allison to the manager's chair, leaving Mercer bitter and hurt by it all. Says Tony Book, the City skipper at that time, 'We knew that there was going to be a change in the boardroom. But most of us just wanted to get on with the football and leave that side of things to others.' Certainly Mercer was keen to keep away from the politics of Maine Road. When several of the players warned him there was going to be trouble, the philosophical Mercer just shrugged his shoulders and told his troops, 'It will all blow over. You just wait and see.'

But one player knew that their manager was adopting the wrong attitude by just sitting on the fence. Francis Lee, who was to prove later that he certainly had a sharp brain for business deals and how to deal with boardroom battles, told Mercer,'You are dead wrong, boss. We all think the world of you. You have got to stand up for yourself. If you don't you will just be pushed out. Mark my words.' Mercer just put on his sheepish grin and muttered, 'Come on, let's talk about football. That's what we are all about.'

Lee's warning had come true and now Mercer had left. Yet several of the directors felt that Mercer's time was up. One who was a great supporter of Allison's promotion to the managership was Ian Niven, a long-standing City director. His devotion to the club and the work he has put into it has been exceptional. Ian runs a smart hotel in Marple Bridge and if you are a City fan and have not visited this establishment then I recommend you to pop in. City's achievements are recalled in photographs and prints on all the walls and Malcolm Allison's face grins at you from all corners. It is a veritable shrine to both the City club and Allison. It is a superb hostelry of which Ian is rightly proud. But looking back to those days of discord, he pours scorn on those who insist it was wrong to remove Mercer from the managership and give Allison his chance. 'Joe had been promising Malcolm he could take over as manager for long enough,' Niven told me. 'Okay, Joe had done a really great job in the early years. But towards the end Malcolm was manager in everything but name. Joe was spending most of his time on the golf course. He should have been happy to step aside and allow Malcolm to have his opportunity that he worked so hard for. Joe wasn't being pushed out of the club. He was just being asked to step aside and let the younger man have what was due to him. He should have been happy to stand back and watch how it went.'

By this time, Peter Swales had been invited to join the board and arbitrate between the two warring factions. Soon he would be chairman. Yet for the moment a new managerial shake-up held everyone's attention.

Ian Niven and his pro-Allison supporters in the City boardroom awaited the start of the 1972-73 season with confidence. But it was not to be the brave new soccer world many of them had forecast. Somehow the absence of the Mercer presence seemed to have taken the gusto out of the City drive. 'It just didn't seem the same,' said Summerbee, 'and it never was again . . .'

Without the influence of Mercer at his side, Malcolm found that the old magic was missing. It wasn't that Allison's great coaching skills were waning but he did find that the heavy responsibilities of being manager of a club as big as Manchester City placed a far greater strain on what one man could achieve. It now came home to Allison just how remarkable had been the extraordinary achievements he and Mercer had pulled off at City. 'In a way, it was like having run a marathon and won it,' recalls Allison. 'And now here we all were trying to do it all over again. There wasn't the same anticipation or challenge there that had been when Joe and I set off together,' he admits frankly.

City started dismally, losing seven of their first ten League matches that season. Clearly, this was to be no title charge in Allison's first spell. City also went out of the UEFA Cup in September, losing 3-4 to Valencia despite Marsh scoring in both legs of the tie. Allison was well aware by now that his rapport with players, while as harmonious as ever, lacked that distinct influence of previous seasons.

The players weren't reacting with the old sparkle. City crashed out of the League Cup, losing 2-0 in the second round to humble near-neighbours Bury in October. Then, in bleak February, there was a fifth round replay 3-1 defeat at Sunderland in the FA Cup which certainly didn't help matters. But Allison was also aware that the boardroom wasn't displaying the solid support of the great Alexander régime which had always backed himself and Joe through thick and thin. Allison says, 'John Humphreys, one of the directors who had helped bring Peter Swales into the boardroom, said to me, "Malcolm, it won't be like before at this great club. It won't be straight up and down any more." He was absolutely right. The atmosphere had changed. The laughs weren't there any more. I felt completely exhausted. I hadn't the same motivation any more and I couldn't relate to the players. I remember Franny Lee warning me, "Don't get involved in the politics at this club." He was dead right. Everyone was trying to get their oar in, trying to influence one player with regards to another. I knew it was time to get out and try to regain my confidence and zest for the game.' Allison quit before the end of the season and took over as manager of Crystal Palace.

How ironic that on 10 March 1973 Joe Mercer reappeared at Maine Road with Coventry City. The City fans gave him a standing ovation and Coventry won 2-1! Revenge is sweet.

Swales sat in his boardroom and meditated. Who should they turn to now? Already the rest of the City board were beginning to realise how dominant their chairman could be in debate and most of all when it came to making the final decision. One director told me, 'He is absolutely brilliant at getting knowledge of a situation from another person and turning it to his advantage. He is so shrewd, he can sway people and he runs the boardroom.'

The board decided to turn to former player and then coach Johnny Hart as his first managerial appointment. Hart had suffered the bitter disappointment of missing his chance to play in an FA Cup final because of an injury in 1955 when Manchester City beat Birmingham City 3-1 at Wembley. He had broken his leg in a game against Huddersfield Town at Leeds Road on 19 March. He had been a forward with City for 18 stolid years before moving on to the coaching staff. His knowledge of the game and popularity with the players was never in question. But shortly after his appointment it became apparent to those close to him that the pressures of the job were already getting too much for him. His close pal and former City midfield man Ken Barnes says, 'It was very sad because Johnny was a great friend of mine. But I and most other people realised it was too much for him. I went into his office once and he literally could not bring himself to decide what team to put out for one particular match. His nerves were badly affected and he was becoming a sick person because of all the tension.'

Hart's loyalty and devotion had taken the toll. Yet in his brief spell at the City helm, Hart brought the famous Denis Law back to Maine Road on a free transfer from Manchester United and also spent £100,000 on Scottish goalkeeper Keith Macrae from Mother-well. In December 1973 Hart quit because of illness. Once again Swales had to ponder on the appointment of a new manager.

Peter Swales and his directors decided it was time to bring in a tough new manager from outside. He wanted a man with a success-ful pedigree in management—one who could stamp his authority on the players and staff and turn Manchester City into a tip-top outfit. Right from the outset in his position in the City boardroom, Swales was acutely aware of the fierce competition from United over at Old Trafford. The man he plumped for was Ron Saunders, then manager of Norwich City. The former Everton striker was doing a good job at Norwich after successful spells with Yeovil and Oxford United. He had taken Norwich to a League Cup final and was regarded highly in the world of soccer. Swales happily paraded his new manager at a press conference. The City chairman said he was completely convinced they now had a manager who was going to take them right to the top of the soccer tree. He pledged his full support for Saunders. City fans were to hear those sort of promises over the years as one manager after another came and went at Maine Road.

Through the years, Peter Swales has spent a large part of his working life trying to make Manchester City a really big and suc-cessful team. His dedication and determination has been enormous. But the fact that City could never recapture the Mercer-Allison glory years must have been galling beyond description for him. He made mistakes but was often quick to admit it. Yet as chairman he could not have spent greater time or have put in more effort in his search for the elusive winning combination to give the fans the success they were craving. It is largely thanks to his untiring efforts that the Maine Road Stadium is one of which the City supporters can take justifiable pride in.

Saunders decided straight away that he was going to be firm. But as he breezed about his business he quickly began to upset both players and staff alike by his brusque style. 'He was a bit of a dictator as far as we were concerned,' says former skipper Ken Barnes, then a coach at Maine Road. 'He was often condescending and always saying "Hello, old man" to everybody on the backroom staff.'

An example of Saunders' lack of tact came when he had the great Denis Law acting almost as a ballboy at the back of goal during training games. The manager had decided the world-famous veteran had no place in his future plans. Yet instead of having a quiet word in Law's ear and even asking his expert views on the rest of the staff—which surely would have been invaluable—Saunders almost ignored him. For the rest of the players and staff to see such treatment of a player who had become a legend in his own lifetime and who was revered in both United and City camps was embarrassing. Many players recall Saunders standing behind them and asking if he was hurting them. When they replied 'No' Saunders told them, 'Well I should be, because I am standing on your hair. Get it cut.' The military approach from the new City boss made the players wonder if they were dealing with a sergeant on the drill square rather than a football manager.

Results were not good. Saunders had a dabble in the transfer market and brought Horswill and the exciting Dennis Tueart from Sunderland to Maine Road, with Tony Towers moving to Roker Park. City even reached the League Cup final but lost 2-1 to Wolves. Meanwhile their League position was once again looking precarious. In March Swales decided to act. He decided to hold a kind of court of inquiry or court martial. He would question all the players to discover if they would support the manager or if they wanted him to go. It was a move that Saunders reacted to bitterly. He felt his chairman had failed to back him up and was quick to say so.

Chapter Ten

IT WAS Tony Book, Saunders' deputy, who instinctively felt that Saunders was going about things in an unfortunate manner. The shrewd Book was alarmed at the aggressive stance Saunders had adopted, 'He was definitely using the sergeant-major approach,' says Book. 'I felt his attitude was wrong because initially he had to win the players over to his side by tact and diplomacy. But he kept saying he was going to turn things round as if he was the only person who counted. He should have appealed to everyone to pull together for the sake of the club. You simply can't handle top professionals like Denis Law, Rodney Marsh, Francis Lee, Colin Bell and Mike Summerbee in the manner that Ron adopted at that time. For remember, we had some of the most experienced internationals in the business at Maine Road.'

Swales had heard that relationships between the manager and his players were strained. Results were going badly and he decided to act. But the method of deciding the fate of Saunders was too much for many people at Maine Road and especially for one player—the frank-speaking Francis Lee.

The City chairman and two other directors decided to hold court in the players' lounge. One by one the players were called into the room and asked to give their opinion of the manager. Not just the first team but some of the young reserve team players were also spoken to by the directors. Clearly Swales had decided to seek a mandate from the playing staff. But everyone at Maine Road recalled what the chairman had said in the City programme at the time he brought in Saunders: 'If he goes down, I go with him.' That was written on 22 December 1973.

Glyn Pardoe and Francis Lee recall the Saunders' Judgment Day with perfect clarity. Says Pardoe, 'All the players were called into the room to tell Swales and the others what they felt about the manager's ability. The whole thing was highly embarrassing. It wasn't the right way to go about things at all regarding a manager's future—no matter what any of us may have felt about him.'

When no-nonsense Lee heard about what was going on in the players' lounge, he went straight up there and told the chairman in no uncertain terms exactly what he thought about the whole business. He told Swales he thought it was an appalling way to go about things regarding a manager's future and that he wanted no part of the whole business. With that he went down to the dressing-room area where Ron Saunders was talking to some members of the staff and evidently was completely unaware that his future was being decided on the floor above. Lee said to him, 'I haven't exactly seen eye to eye with you since you came here, but what is going on up there in the lounge is a disgrace and I want you to know I will have no part in it. I just wanted you to know that.'

Saunders was shocked at what had been going on, yet was powerless to stop it. The inexorable Swales axe fell on Saunders' neck and that was that. So after only five months in the job, Saunders found himself out of work. He couldn't help reminding people what Swales had said when he appointed him. 'He said he would back me all the way, yet within no time at all he just walked away.'

Saunders, by his abrasive style, certainly hadn't made many friends and had certainly upset plenty of people during his short stay. But his argument had been that Swales had brought him into the club to straighten it out and rule with a rod of iron. Yet when some of the players had got into a rebellious mood, Swales had failed to back the captain of his ship.

But let us find out for the first time the true manner of Saunders' sacking. Saunders spoke to me quite frankly when I asked him to give me the details of just how Peter Swales delivered the bullets. 'I was called to his house at eight o'clock in the morning. The funny thing was that you might have thought you had been called for a pat on the back rather than the other,' added Saunders. 'He told me he had decided he had to dismiss me. I was stunned. Yet, looking back, not surprised. For that short time at Maine Road, nothing could really surprise me. There were so many people interfering and trying to influence things, you never knew what was coming next. But when Swales told me I was finished after such a short time and after having brought me in to sort things out MY way, I was just completely baffled by the man. And what he said next left me even more nonplussed. He said, "I am probably making the biggest mistake of my life in dismissing you and I know it."' Saunders looked the City chairman straight in the eye and said, 'You could be right there.'

Several directors recalled at the moment of Saunders' shock dismissal that only a matter of months earlier, on appointing him, Swales had said, 'We have got the man who will be the best manager in the business.' From the very first day he moved into the manager's office at Maine Road, Saunders had shown that he was a caring husband and father. On the day he left that office for the last time, two players were present when he proudly lifted the photograph of his wife and children from the desk to take with him. 'Thank God I've got these to go home to,' said Ron. 'At least they are loyal.'

It is to Saunders' eternal credit that he walked away from this extraordinary treatment with only one thing in his mind. It was not revenge for the harsh sentence City had handed out. Ron Saunders had fierce pride in his own ability and he was going to prove the judgment woefully wrong. He moved eventually to Aston Villa and the next season won the League Cup and steered them skilfully to promotion to the First Division. He was voted Manager of the Year. If Swales and the rest of the City board wriggled with embarrassment, then it was nothing to what happened five years later when Saunders built Villa with patient and skilful handling into the best team in England. They took the First Division championship and Saunders was the hero of Villa Park. He had proved his excellence—his ability as a manager was now unquestioned.

Villa were exuberant. They had taken on a manager in Saunders, given him full financial support and, most of all, the necessary time to produce the power and class to build a championship team. Saunders had done it with style and determination. Yet Saunders refuses to vilify Swales for the treatment he received in that brief stay at Maine Road. 'I remember listening as Swales said he felt he could be making the biggest mistake of his life in sacking me, and suddenly realising why he was in football. He is like so many other chairmen. They don't understand football at all. Yet they want to be in it,' he told me. 'They want to have the reflected glory. It is actually rather sad. I don't feel anything against Peter Swales. I feel sorry for him, because he is trying to be head of something he will never begin to understand the working of. Football is beyond him. That's the most telling thing in the whole business.'

The City board next turned to former skipper Tony Book to solve their managerial problem. Book's attitude on taking the hot seat was to play it cool. He told the players they were all in it together and they must work together. Book says today, 'Unity was everything as far as I was concerned. I felt there was wonderful talent within the City playing squad at that time. Equally, the fans had been brilliant in their support. What I wanted was complete dedication and effort. There was the nucleus of a team that could win the championship if we had the one hundred per cent drive that was needed.'

It was a remarkable position for the former bricklayer from the West Country to find himself in. 'When I was given the chance as a full-back for City at the age of 32, I thought quite simply, "Well, this is great at my age. I'll give it all I have." But I never expected to last more than a year. I was convinced it was a 12-month wonder. Yet I had lasted many more years as a player and won every honour in the game. It had been a situation beyond my wildest dreams. I loved Manchester, the fans, the whole situation. Yet now here I was being offered the managership. It was something I had to go for. I was determined to give Manchester City every ounce of effort I could as a manager. It would be like returning their kindness in the way they had welcomed me into the camp in those first exciting days.'

Book was to recompense that kindness of the fans with some of the finest and most astute managerial performances the club has enjoyed in the last 20 years. But, like all the others, he was handicapped at vital moments by the board of directors who never gave their manager the full support he deserved in his bid for success.

Book was in charge of the City team that had to go to Old Trafford on that final fixture of the 1973-74 season knowing that victory would condemn the old enemy to relegation to the Second Division. Tommy Docherty's United side had struggled all season. But still the Reds' supporters believed they would escape the drop in this derby battle. Indeed it looked as if they might survive until the 82nd minute when in one of the greatest ironies the ball was back-heeled over the United line for the winner by ex-United hero Denis Law. Despite the congratulations from his fellow City players who swarmed around him, Law walked back looking a little crestfallen . . . as if he hadn't really got any enjoyment from the goal. 'Yes, I was unhappy,' he says today. 'I knew as the ball reached me that it would mean a great club like United would be destined to the Second Division and it made me very sad. I had spent the major part of my career at Old Trafford and it was a sad moment to think I was playing a part in sending them down.' But it was a triumph for Book's management style in his first derby and the Blues' fans were delighted. They suddenly felt Book was the man to get back to the sort of soccer City had produced in his great playing days when the sky was the limit for the club.

CHAPTER ELEVEN

THE QUIET MAN of Maine Road . . . that was Tony Book. But although City's new manager was to be undemonstrative in comparison to the flamboyant style of the Mercer-Allison days, Book was nonetheless determined his team would have dash and style. 'I wanted to give the fans what they really wanted—a team who had quality and who could attack and give them the sort of soccer that they had become accustomed to at Manchester City.' And, among the many managers to come and go during chairman Peter Swales' 20-year rule, he was to be the ONLY manager to win a trophy. But for a decision to sell one of City's greatest players it could well have been that Book would have landed the First Division championship he so desperately longed for.

Before the opening of that 1974 season, Book lost the services of Francis Lee. Many at Maine Road at that time believe the decision to sell Lee was taken at boardroom level and that Book, like many other managers to come after him, had to 'obey orders'. Before the transfer went through, Lee saw Peter Swales and told him bluntly, 'You will regret the day you sold me. I promise you that.' But what Lee was not to know at that time was that another club was ready to compete with Derby County, for whom Lee eventually signed. That club was none other than arch-rival and neighbour Manchester United. Their then dynamic manager Tommy Docherty had been tipped off that Lee was to leave Maine Road. The Doc knew a top player like Lee would be a godsend to him. He immediately contacted City but was told bluntly, 'Yes, Lee is going to be transferred, but there is no way we would let him go to United.' That was the end of Doc's hopes of signing Lee whom he regarded as still the best striker in the business.

There was no more delighted a man at the start of the season than Dave Mackay who snapped up Lee, still only 30 years old, for £100,000. The decision to sell Lee was a disastrous mistake by City and no one in the 40,000 crowd will ever forget Lee's stunning return in the Derby County team, on 28 December 1974. The score was 1-1 with the game finely balanced. There was only a minute to go. It looked as if someone had to produce something pretty special to break the impasse. That someone was to be Lee. He took the ball out on the left of goal, cut in steadily and, moving the ball on to his right foot, sent a blazing drive searing into the roof of the net from 25 yards out. It was probably the best goal seen at Maine Road that season and the BBC *Match of the Day* cameras were there to capture the dramatic moment that left Peter Swales, his fellow directors and poor manager Tony Book cringing with embarrassment. The magnificent City fans showed just how sporting they are and how much they still felt for their former hero. They rose to give a truly remarkable ovation to that great strike. Lee recalls, 'I was naturally delighted to make a point. But the reaction of those City fans was nothing short of magnificent. They made my afternoon, and I can never thank them enough for their wonderful spontaneous reaction to that goal.'

Those prophetic words of Lee to chairman Swales that he would regret selling him were even further emphasised when City lost 2-1 to Derby County at the Baseball Ground which meant that Derby County marched on to lift the championship—Lee's second championship medal, to go with the one he won with City under Mercer and Allison.

One of Book's most important signings was brought in before the start of the 1974-75 season. He wanted a player with real flair and power in the midfield to add an extra dimension to their attacking strength. The man he went for was Scottish international Asa Hartford. City paid West Bromwich Albion £250,000 for the 23-year-old Hartford. It was a bold decision by Book. Hartford had made dramatic headlines in 1972 when he looked all set to join high-flying Leeds United in a £170,000 deal. But during a medical examination prior to the transfer going through, a specialist for Leeds United declared that Hartford suffered from a hole in the heart condition. This, in his opinion, placed Hartford's whole football future in jeopardy. It was a stunning blow to Hartford and despite Leeds manager Don Revie doing his best to console the young Scot, Hartford felt at that moment in time that his world had come to an end. But he refused to accept the verdict.

Hartford had come straight into English soccer from Scottish amateur football, when he had joined West Bromwich Albion from Drumchapel Amateurs after manager Jimmy Hagan had received rave reports about the midfield terrier with the fearsome, biting tackles and a nose for goals. But now his career seemed over. 'Revie could hardly bring himself to tell me the news,' says Hartford. 'I will never forget his face as the tears started to run down his cheeks. He was very emotional and he clearly felt that he was telling me it was the death sentence to my career.' Yet this tough, durable little Scot had no intention of taking the news as gospel. 'Everyone was upset for me and consoling me when I got back to West Brom. Manager Don Howe was fabulous and insisted I was to have further examinations with specialists picked by the club. I was 21 and I felt terrific, and I was determined to play on and have a happy and long career,' he says. 'I was never breathless. I felt there was nothing to stop me.'

Two further specialist checks were made and the final verdict was that, although he had a tiny pinprick hole in the heart, this would in no way prevent Asa enjoying a career in professional football. 'I was overjoyed yet irritated to think that I had missed the chance of getting into the First Division with Leeds, as West Brom were in the Second Division. My chance to go to Leeds would have been the perfect solution for my ambitions,' Hartford recalls.

His determination to leave Albion led to some stormy scenes between the fiery Hartford and the club. But he got his move in August 1974 when Book moved in and beat Wolves to snap him up for £250,000.

Book also decided he needed a first-class deputy. He wanted a top coach, but also somebody who would add a bit of fire and excitement to the City camp. In a way Book, the quiet, steady man of football, felt he wanted a live-wire number two. He was rather following in Mercer's footsteps when Joe had plumped for the out-going Allison to be his deputy. Book turned to the valuable Scot and former Middlesbrough man, Ian McFarlane, with whom he had built up a firm friendship when they were players at Bath City together.

'Ian had a wonderful, fiery temperament,' says Book. 'I felt he would be the ideal man to work with me at City. We had the same ideas and attitudes to the sort of football we wanted to see our team play. I felt Ian was just the man to give the team that extra bit of drive and colour. In a way, I felt he could give them a good kick up the backside when it was called for in training. In a word, he could knock them down and it would be me who would pick them up again,' he laughed.

Book had plenty of well-seasoned campaigners to call on in his first season of management. New arrival Hartford found he was rubbing shoulders with top players like the colourful Rodney Marsh and goal-getter Dennis Tueart, while the great Colin Bell and Mike Summerbee were still there. Alan Oakes was now a formidable force in midfield and Joe Corrigan was showing himself to be a classy goalkeeper. But also there were several exciting young players coming through—notably winger Peter Barnes and midfield young-ster Gary Owen. Barnes was the son of former skipper and midfield ace Ken Barnes. He had a truly exceptional gift of being able to beat defenders in long, effortless runs, either down the flanks or through the middle. Owen was equally exciting with his astute midfield skills. Obviously they were two players with a great future.

It proved to be a quiet season with City finishing a creditable eighth in the First Division after making early exits in the Cup competitions. They went out in the third round of the FA Cup, losing 2-0 to Newcastle United. They had been dismissed from the League Cup in the third round by old adversaries Manchester United, who licked them 1-0 at Old Trafford thanks to a Gerry Daly penalty.

But by now Book had bought big striker Joe Royle from Everton for £170,000. The following season Book felt confident. 'We were playing with a lot of purpose and flair,' he remembers. 'I felt we were well capable of winning something and sure enough so it was to prove.' It was the League Cup that grabbed the attention of the City fans as Book's team moved powerfully through the early rounds of the competition in that 1975-76 season.

The second round had been a monumental struggle with Norwich City. The first match ended in a 1-1 draw at Norwich and then they finished all square at 2-2 in the replay at Maine Road. But after winning the toss for venue City crushed the Canaries 6-1 at Stamford Bridge on 29 September. Dennis Tueart grabbed a hat-trick.

84

The third round was a home tie against Nottingham Forest which City won 2-1. A huge roar of excitement erupted in both Maine Road and Old Trafford camps when the draw for the next round proclaimed the fourth round on 12 November meant United had to come to City's ground to do battle once more. In the words of Peter Barnes, 'We hammered them off the park.' City walloped the Reds 4-0 despite losing Colin Bell with a dreadful knee injury that effectively ended his star-studded career.

The fifth round saw City drawn against Mansfield Town at home and again the goals flowed in a 4-2 victory. This meant a semi-final battle with—of all clubs as far as McFarlane was concerned—Middlesbrough. The build-up for this semi-final was packed with tension. Barnes recalls, 'We were in the middle of a training session when we heard Ian shouting, "You'll never be a player." Some of the lads took exception and next thing all hell was let loose. It ended with Tony and Ian squaring up to one another, only for the rest of the players to break it up. It was just sheer emotion before the big match. But it was over in a minute or two and then everyone was laughing. It was just the sort of explosion of tension you get in the build-up to a big game.'

McFarlane was proving the exact stimulant Book had believed he could be when he brought him to Maine Road. Says Barnes, 'The younger players loved him. He was full of confidence and made them think they could be world-beaters. He had not got time for personalities. Yet his earthiness got through to everyone. Ian was a team man, simple as that. That was why Book got him. It was a matter of everyone being important—not just the better known players.'

The semi-final struggle with Middlesbrough was a two-leg affair at that time and when 'Boro won the first leg 1-0 at Ayresome Park, their fans were confident they were on the way to Wembley. Boss Jackie Charlton wrote in the programme for the second leg: 'It will be a tight game—there won't be many goals.' He was right about that—as far as Middlesbrough were concerned. City crushed them 4-0 with goals coming from Alan Oakes, Ged Keegan, Peter Barnes and Joe Royle.

So the big day loomed. McFarlane's move from Middlesbrough to City looked a winner. Yet the incorrigible McFarlane was to play an extraordinary role in City's stunning success in the League Cup final. But that will follow later. In the build-up to the final, City's squad was taken to a health farm at Tring. All seemed full of brimming confidence. But Book suddenly found he had a massive problem—key defender Dave Watson had a serious back problem. Book went to see what the trouble was with his vital link-man. To his horror, he found the most important player in his plans lying on his back. Book stood there and felt his world was coming apart. 'I said to Dave, "You must have no chance of playing in the final." But he grinned at me and said, "Don't worry, I'll be there." I could not believe him. Yet I respected his attitude as a professional. I knew he would not give me empty promises. Nevertheless, at that moment, seeing him lying on the floor of his chalet, I still feared the worst. It was a difficult moment. You have to make the decision, but equally you rely on a player's honesty. In this case, Dave was superb. He had a great final.'

Later, Watson was to have an operation on his spine. But on this occasion he braced himself against pain and untold agonies to guide City to their one trophy triumph in the Swales chairmanship. It was a final with an extraordinary build-up as far as City were concerned. Once again it was the wild McFarlane who set the adventurous mood that was to help guide City to victory.

'When we trooped out for the start in front of a crowd of 100,000,' says Barnes, 'we suddenly realised there was an extra player in our party. At that time we wore huge track suits, rather like the awful Ku Klux Klan. With a hood pulled over your head it was difficult to pick out who was who. But as we started the kick around before the final, we realised Ian was out there with us—shooting in at Joe Corrigan's goal. He was loving it and bawled out, "I've done it. I've played at Wembley."'

Says Corrigan: 'Ian was a wonderful coach and motivator. But he was as mad as a March hare sometimes. Once, when I was in his car as he drove down the motorway, he was grumbling about how he had just a humble make of a car while Allison had been going around in a Jaguar. "Tell me who is the better coach, big man," he demanded. I said I felt that Malcolm just had the edge. With that he almost pulled to a halt in the fast lane and it was a wonder we weren't both killed,' says Joe. 'I quickly said: "Okay, you were." And happily he drove on.'

Skipper Mike Doyle remembers McFarlane's pre-match antics at Wembley and laughs, 'He had walked out behind Tony Book and then stayed on the pitch. It was typical of Ian. But he was 100 per cent behind the players and they loved him.' Barnes reckons, 'That bit of tomfoolery put us in the right mood and we were all relaxed by the time he had been persuaded to leave.' Recalls Dennis Tueart, who was to have an unforgettable final, 'I said, "For God's sake, get off the pitch before someone sees what's going on."'

So the final was on and the boast of Newcastle's big centre-forward Malcolm MacDonald–'This is going to be our big day'–was put to the test. It was City who struck the first blow. A clever free kick by Asa Hartford was flicked across to the far post by the cunning Doyle. Peter Barnes darted in to flash a volley home and send the hordes of blue and white supporters into wild scenes of jubilation. But just before half-time Newcastle were level. It was MacDonald who set up the chance for Alan Gowling to equalise. But during the half-time break, Book was still confident. 'I felt we had the class to finish it. The lads were full of determination and I was always sure it would be our day.'

So it was to prove. But for Tueart it was to be possibly the greatest moment of his career. Just after half-time, he produced the killer shot to break Newcastle's hearts—and what a sensational goal it was. It must rank as one of the greatest ever seen on Wembley's historic turf. Willie Donachie, always a key player in so many great City matches, crossed a great ball to Tommy Booth. The big defender headed across the face of goal and Tueart produced a spectacular bicycle-kick to send the ball flashing into the roof of the net. Wembley erupted in acclaim of a staggering goal.

Says Tueart modestly as he remembers that glittering moment, 'When Tommy headed across, I had actually gone past the flight of the ball. But I just instinctively fell and struck an overhead kick towards goal. I just happened to catch it well and I suppose it was pretty spectacular. I was just glad it went in. But although that goal is still talked about I did no more than all the other lads in that final. It was a team triumph.'

There was a personal disappointment for big striker Joe Royle who had a goal disallowed for offside. That would have made the score 3-1 had it been allowed to stand in the second half. 'I scored in every round and that would have been the icing on the cake as far as I was concerned,' says Royle, now the highly impressive manager of Oldham Athletic. 'I darted through and chipped the ball over the goalkeeper but I was certain I was onside. It was a bit of a disappointment from my point of view, but all that mattered really was the team had triumphed and won the League Cup.'

Doyle skipped joyfully up the Wembley steps and held aloft the only major trophy City fans were to see from that day to this.

The Wembley triumph over Newcastle United was soured for Book when his bubbling aide McFarlane announced he was quitting Manchester City. Once again the City board failed to act positively to keep a winning management team together. McFarlane had some personal problems and had sought the financial aid of the City club by asking them to give him a loan regarding some property he needed to buy. But City's reaction, despite the success they were enjoying at that time, which was bringing extra revenue into the club, was to turn him down. McFarlane felt bitterly hurt and made his decision to quit. 'It was a blow to lose him,' says Book. 'He had a wonderful effect on the players in the dressing-room and he was a great coach. He had proved his worth in the way the results had gone. But when his mind was made up there was nothing I could do about it.' So Book had to look around for a successor. He decided to ask advice from one of the shrewdest soccer brains in the business—the former City forward and successful manager of Leeds United, Don Revie. The recommendation from Revie was to take on Bill Taylor, the highly rated Fulham coach who also had a role as one of the coaches in the England squad. So Taylor, a quiet and unobtrusive man, arrived at Maine Road at a time of great promise for Book's squad.

The season of 1976-77 was to be City's biggest drive for the coveted League Championship since the Mercer days. Certainly there was an abundance of experience, youth and talent packed into City's ranks as they set out on the title trail that season. Book pulled off a shrewd signing in the close season when he paid Arsenal £100,000 for former Manchester United striker Brian Kidd. United had transferred the Manchester-born Kidd to Arsenal for £110,000 in August 1974. Book had always been a great admirer of Kidd and was delighted to have snapped him up at last. 'Brian was a tremendous competitor,' says Book. 'He would always get goals for you and I knew he was still as hungry as ever despite having been with two big clubs like United and Arsenal already. Kidd would get me goals, I was fully confident of that.' Kidd was delighted to be back in Manchester and seized his new opportunity with a zest that delighted Book. The goals flowed from his boots. He was to share the attack with big Joe Royle and Book says, 'Joe was an expert when it came to getting goals. He was the gentle giant. If he had had a bit of a mean streak and a little more steel he would really have made the sparks fly. Don't get me wrong, he was a heck of a good striker, but I felt there was the ability for him to have been even greater, maybe another Dixie Dean. But I couldn't have asked for more than he gave.'

But there was a big disappointment for Book that season. He felt he had to strengthen his hand still further to give the title chances an even impetus. He wanted to sign a new man to make up for the loss of the great Colin Bell through injury. Bell was still fighting his way down a long, painful road to recovery after seriously damaging his knee in the derby match against United the previous season when City beat them 4-0 in the fourth round of the League Cup at Maine Road. The man Book saw as the vital player who could give them a really great chance of the championship was that little master tactician, Alan Ball, of Arsenal and England. But when it came to the crunch, Book was told that the board could not see their way to paying out big money for Ball. So the City manager had to shrug his shoulders and get on with the job. Book still believes that Ball would have made the difference needed to take the title. 'Ball was the one man I needed,' says Book.

Yet City had a terrific crack at it. Book recalls a vital moment that cost them the title. 'It came when we played Liverpool in December at Maine Road. We were going great guns and I thought that if we could win against Liverpool, it would give us the vital impetus to take the title.' Liverpool were top of the First Division with City lying in third place. There was a crowd of 50,020 at Maine Road on 29 December 1976 to see the battle. Liverpool had brought in Jimmy Case as their brilliant Kevin Keegan was out through an injury. It was a frosty pitch and the players had trouble keeping their feet at times. But City struck a vital blow when Joe Royle gave them the lead. It looked to be City's day. Then with only two minutes left, disaster struck for Book's men. Centre-half Dave Watson, who was always in the thick of the battle, lost his footing on the icy pitch and as he was harassed by David Fairclough—and to the horror of the almost disbelieving City fans—he turned the ball past goalkeeper Joe Corrigan. The Liverpool fans hooted with delight, yet no one in that jam-packed Maine Road crowd could know at that time that Watson's bad luck on the frozen pitch meant Liverpool had grabbed a point—remember, it was the days of two points for a win and one for a draw—that being the slim difference between them taking the title and City having to settle for the runners-up spot.

The wisdom of Book's purchase of Kidd was illustrated vividly in the next League game against Leicester City. Brian hit home four goals in the 5-0 victory, Mike Doyle adding the other. He was the first City man to strike in four—without penalties—since Fred Tilson had achieved it on 26 November 1932 against Aston Villa whom City beat 5-2.

City had little luck in any of the Cup competitions. Juventus put them out of the UEFA Cup, the Blues winning 1-0 at home but going down 0-2 in Italy. They were beaten 3-0 by Aston Villa at Villa Park in the second round of the League Cup. But they fared better in the FA Cup, beating West Brom 1-0 in a third round replay at the Hawthorns after a 1-1 draw at Maine Road. After an impressive 3-1 win at Newcastle in the next round, another away tie in the fifth round at Leeds United proved their undoing as they went down by the only goal of the game.

Nonetheless, Book was rightly proud of the season in which they had come so close to lifting the championship to crown all his efforts of trying to bring back the Mercer and Allison lustre to the Maine Road club. 'I was proud of the way the team were playing,' says Book. 'Although we had a well-organised defence, the team were attacking and giving a lot of excitement. It had colour all the way through the side.' The aggressive Doyle, so far an explosive, attacking midfielder, had now shown his versatility by cementing a defensive partnership in the middle of City's rearguard. Book had constructed a formidable defence, for City conceded only 34 League goals—a proud club record in that 1976-77 season.

Before the opening of the next season Tony Book decided he wanted a new man to boost his striking power. The player he turned to was Southampton's lanky genial England ace, Mick Channon. He paid a then club record of £300,000 for Channon who welcomed the chance to play a role with a renowned club like Manchester City. But in fairness to Peter Swales and Book, Southampton were not keen to part with him and it took a lot of money and a lot of persuasion to land Channon at Maine Road. The likeable Channon, always with a happy grin on his face, insisted he wasn't purely a striker when he held his first chat with the press on signing for City. 'I feel there is more to my game than just scoring goals,' he maintained. 'I think that City, with the top quality they have at Maine Road, are going to give me the real challenge I have been looking for. I have no regrets about leaving Southampton, although

I had 13 happy years there. But I felt it was time for me to move and try something new and City looks an exciting, new opportunity.' As Channon came in, the genial, big Joe Royle realised it was time for him to move on. The highly popular Royle recalls, 'I knew it was a case of my going to a new club. You have to accept it. I realised that Tony wanted to try a new attacking partnership with Channon and Brian Kidd and, although I was obviously disappointed, I had to accept it. City's number two, Bill Taylor, was keen for me to stay and I felt that if I went somewhere on loan there might be a change in the situation. Tony asked me if I would go on loan to Bristol City. So I went.'

Talk about making an impact in your first match! On his debut at Bristol, Royle hammered in four cracking goals and it didn't take much longer for a deal to be agreed between Bristol and Maine Road for a permanent £100,000 worth of Royle. 'I was sorry to go,' says Royle, who was still only 28. 'City had so many wonderful people on the staff, from the tea ladies to the coaching staff. But somehow, it never seemed to be quite right at the top. There always seemed to be shadows in corridors. Most people felt that things were never quite right in the boardroom.'

City flew from the starting blocks in the 1977-78 season. They were unbeaten in their first eight games, winning five of them. One of those victories was a 3-1 triumph over big rivals United at Maine Road and Book must have been thrilled to see his new strike pair hit it off in a big way as Kidd grabbed two goals and Channon the other. Equally impressive was the 4-1 win at Villa Park with Tueart scoring the first of three League hat-tricks he would get that season. But then things went wrong, with four defeats coming in the next six matches and Channon out for a spell through injury. Then in December they won four of five games and looked back in the title hunt with a vengeance.

1978 had only just started when Book had to face the shock of Dennis Tueart being determined to move from Maine Road. The astute Tueart realised it was a perfect time for him to move on and he was shrewd enough to know where he wanted to go. So when he was told Manchester United wanted to buy him, he shook everybody in Manchester by saying he wasn't interested. Tueart, who has proved since his playing days were over that he has a shrewd business brain, had already decided that he wanted to play abroad. But it was not on the Continent. It was in the United States.

Sure enough, his move went ahead when the New York Cosmos, the leading club in the North America League, paid up £250,000 for his services—a record fee paid by an American club for a League club player. Looking back, Tueart says, 'I loved my time at Maine Road. I thought the team that won the League Cup against Newcastle and those under Tony Book afterwards gave City fans their best years since the Mercer era. Certainly I felt that we might have won the championship in the 1976-77 season, when Liverpool pipped us by a point, if we had had maybe one or two top-flight players to just strengthen the side. But I felt Book was the man for the job and it was a mistake to take the position away from him in the end.'

Certainly, all the star players in League football who were earning top wages in the soccer world at that time must have turned green with envy on learning in the press that Tueart was reported to be able to earn over £1,000 a week in the States as a result of his clever transfer—a fortune at that time.

But there was to be no replacement for Tueart as the season progressed, despite there being a hefty £250,000 in the Maine Road coffers to buy another man to strengthen Book's hand. After Tueart departed for the States in February 1978, City slumped with only one victory in a dismal eight-match spell. They were knocked out of the FA Cup, losing 2-1 away to Nottingham Forest. In the League Cup they fared a little better, going out 1-0 to Arsenal at Highbury in a fifth round replay after a goalless draw in the original tie at Maine Road. Nonetheless, City ended in a creditable fourth place in the First Division. Had another top-flight player been brought in to make up for the absence of the wily Tueart, who knows how much closer Book might have been to that elusive title? Yet Book was clearly a little disappointed in his big buy, Channon. The reliable Kidd had come up with 20 goals. 'But I'm sorry to say I feel Mick disappointed me most,' says Book. 'I felt he had more to offer than he managed to produce. He seemed to spend most of his time on his backside. A player with exceptional ability when at his very best, but through that period at City he never produced the football I knew he was well capable of. It was just one of those things.'

CHAPTER TWELVE

BOOK'S FIRST disappointing moment arrived in the middle of the 1978–79 campaign. City had drawn three and lost one in their opening four-match spell. But then a jaunty charge that brought five wins from the next six games seemed to suggest that Book had got the train back on the rails and was building up a nice head of steam. Yet from mid-October, City failed to win any of their remaining 11 League games that year and were also knocked out of the League Cup, losing 2-1 at Southampton. Funnily enough, City were only losing by the odd goal in low scoring games. But it was the attack of Mike Channon and Brian Kidd which was not showing the fire-power Book had banked on. This slump was enough to set the alarm bells ringing in the Maine Road corridors of power.

Once again, the men in the boardroom were restless for change. The new strategy that was adopted was to startle the football world. It was Ian Niven who put it to Swales and the rest of the directors. 'The only answer to our problems is to bring back Malcolm Allison.' Some directors were adamantly against the suggestion. But while Swales usually went his own way once he had reached his own decision, the Allison idea intrigued him. If anyone had the ability to influence his thinking it was the quietly spoken Niven. Hadn't Allison been the architect of all the great achievements in the glorious '70s? Malcolm had the drive and flair to build a great team again.

He had been tired and bored before he quit and left to join Crystal Palace, said Niven. In fact, Allison had had a dull five years by his high standards since leaving Maine Road. He had quit Palace,

coached on the Continent and then the United States, before returning to Plymouth Argyle, the original club he had managed just
before joining Joe Mercer at Maine Road. Now he was itching to
make a return to big-time football and Niven was well aware of
it. The scheme appealed to Swales. Maybe Allison could weave his
special brand of magic for a second time around. So, on a sharp
January morning, Allison stepped back through the famous portals
of Maine Road with a broad grin on his face and the inevitable cigar
clamped between his jaws. He was now 51 years old, but looked as
trim and as fit as ever. Tony Book had felt that he and his coach Bill
Taylor were doing a good enough job as it was. 'The team wasn't in
any danger of relegation, and I felt things were going along quite
nicely,' Book says today. 'But when they decided to bring back
Malcolm, I just had to accept it.'

But when Allison arrived everyone in the club was in for a shock.
He may have looked the same, the bold extrovert of the earlier
years at Maine Road. But this was not the same man. 'It certainly
wasn't the Malcolm I had known as a player under him in the great
days,' recalls Book. 'He hadn't the same confidence. He wasn't
relaxed, and seemed tense and a little unsure of quite what he
wanted to do.'

Certainly, Book was a little apprehensive. If ever an introvert
was now teamed with an extrovert, this was it. Book could be bold
in his own way. But in the management game Book was shrewd,
careful and wont to give himself the option of second thoughts on a
particular deal or plan of strategy. Allison arrived for his second
term at Maine Road with an immediate plan—to build a new team
of exciting young players who would be the future from which
Manchester City could go forward to new successes. Book, naturally upset that Swales and the board should have decided things
were going wrong, recalls the Allison return with disappointment,
though not with rancour. 'Malcolm had always wanted to be seen
as the disciple, building a new team,' he says. 'But on this occasion
he went at it too quickly, without giving enough thought as to
exactly what was involved and what the implications of his rather
rash decisions might be. In my opinion, he rushed players in and
out of the side without the real thought of what they were really
capable of and what they were worth. It was a kind of hit or miss
business. At this time in his career, although I had had tremendous
times with him and admired his bravado as much as anyone in the

past, I was disappointed by his lack of patience. This was, after all, a vital point in the club's future.' But there was to be an added complication to the new Book-Allison combination as they struggled to head the City ship away from the rocks and reorganise a baffled crew. For as Book and Allison argued on the best course to take and the new players to buy to strengthen the side, it became apparent to both of them that decisions were being taken in the boardroom on which players were vital to City's cause and also their worth—even if it was far above the prices already set by Book and Allison.

One of the most controversial decisions taken during this Book-Allison liaison came before the start of the 1979-80 season. It was the decision to sell first Gary Owen and then Peter Barnes to West Bromwich Albion. Both were popular players with the Maine Road fans and both had started as youngsters at the club, rising to become established and popular first-team men. Barnes was already an England international winger of exceptional skill and the midfield wizardry of Owen had won him England Under-23 caps. Owen was the first to go, on 30 May 1979. He was almost in tears at the decision and said, 'It is a terrific wrench to leave Maine Road. It has been like home. But if the club don't want me to stay, there is nothing else for it and I shall have to do my best for West Brom.' Two months later, Barnes followed his pal Owen to the Midlands when he also signed for the Hawthorns club. Recalling those shock moves, Barnes says today, 'It was amazing luck that City got Gary as a youngster in the first place. As a boy, he was a dyed-in-the-wool Red, having always followed Manchester United. He nearly signed for United, for he was due to go for talks with the then manager Frank O'Farrell on the recommendation of chief scout John Aston. But United dismissed O'Farrell before young Gary could have his big chance and City stepped in.' City seemed to have signed two heavenly soccer twins—everyone in football was then impressed by Barnes and Owen. Even the great Bobby Charlton of United and England fame remarked, 'They have the soccer world at their feet.' But the way it worked out on Allison's return, their Manchester City lives were over. Says Peter, 'I spoke to my dad and he was as mystified as I was about it. I was 21 and already an England player yet City had no further want of me. Okay, I had been left out a little earlier and I had even said if I wasn't in the first team I wanted to go. But I never thought it would come to that. And yet, when I look back, I could see that the team was disintegrating. Dave Watson had gone to Werder Bremen and Asa Hartford had moved to Nottingham Forest. There didn't seem to be any logic in it.'

Nevertheless, Barnes and Owen left and Allison pressed on with more transfers. By this time Brian Kidd had left for Everton to be replaced when Allison brought in the colourful Barry Silkman from Plymouth Argyle. He was quite a gifted ball player. But again, most City followers felt that Kidd was going to be difficult to replace considering his high return of goals over a season.

Most of all, Allison is bitterly angry at the insinuations that he was ready to pay highly inflated prices for players. The biggest block-busting signing at that time in football was Steve Daley from Wolves. City had been stalking Daley for a long time. The Wolverhampton club and manager were fascinated at City's seemingly stop-at-nothing determination to land Daley. City were flat out to get this midfield player most people in the game were hailing as a world-beater. But Allison insists that the bidding got wildly out of control. He is adamant that once the fee reached £750,000 he recommended to chairman Swales that that was as far as they should go. Book agrees totally. 'That was as high as we should have gone as far as I was concerned,' says Book. 'Both Malcolm and myself were ready to shrug our shoulders, call it a day and look elsewhere.' But the City board made it clear Daley was to be pursued. Allison readily con-cedes he was highly impressed by Daley. He reveals, 'I had been interested in Daley for some time. I saw Wolves manager John Barnwell at a training session at Lilleshall. I asked John how much he wanted and he replied £750,000. I said I would give him £600,000. But he dug his heels in. I left it at that. Then John was in a car accident, and later, when I made another inquiry, Ritchie Barker was in charge. Again I offered £600,000 but, like Barnwell, Ritchie said they wanted £750,000. Then, when we were on our way to a match at Southampton, Tony told me after speaking to Swales, "We've paid £1.1 million for Daley. He will be joining us." I said as far as I was concerned, I didn't want to sign him if he was going to cost as much as that. But it was done.' Daley signed on 5 September 1979.

At the start of the 1979-80 season there were still some long-serving players on hand to be called upon. Scottish international Willie Donachie had the left full-back spot practically on his own without a break since first joining the senior side in the 1972-73 season. He played 35 times for Scotland and made 347 senior

Howard Kendall enjoying a welcome cup of tea on the day he was appointed manager of Manchester City

Future chairman Francis Lee is mobbed by jubilant fans

Paul Walsh scoring his first goal for City since signing from Portsmouth for £750,000 during the 3–0 win over Aston Villa (above) and being congratulated by his new team-mates (below)

Uwe Rosler celebrating his first goal for the club, against Aston Villa, since joining them on loan from Borussia Dortmund

Francis Lee gives a welcome kiss to Norah Mercer, widow of the great former City manager Joe Mercer. Also pictured is former City and England star Colin Bell, now a coach with the club.

Syd Little and Eddie Large – big City fans and Francis Lee supporters – share a joke with former City and England forward Mike Summerbee as they wait for Lee to appear as the new chairman. Francis Lee's son, Gary, is on Little's left

The moment of victory. Francis Lee, the new chairman, receives a huge ovation from the 28,000 crowd at Maine Road before the game against Ipswich on 5 February 1994

Lee's despondency is obvious as Ian Marshall gives Ipswich a 1–0 lead at Maine Road

Lee and his ally and director Colin Barlow cheer Gary Flitcroft's thrilling goal as City recover to beat Ipswich 2–1

City defender David Brightwell blasts home City's winner against high-flying Newcastle (above) and is congratulated by Paul Walsh and Peter Beagrie (below)

A goal at the wrong end for City fans as Newcastle's Scott Sellars slips the ball past Andy Dibble to give his team the lead

It looks as though City's Paul Walsh can't fail to score, but Newcastle keeper Pavel Srnicek gets across to block with the help of Scott Sellars

Peter Beagrie, Manchester City's new £1.3 million signing from Everton, in action against Aston Villa

Uwe Rosler holding off a challenge from Tony Daley of Aston Villa

appearances for City. He was utterly cool under pressure and was a great passer of the ball, especially with his cultured left boot. This was to be his last season with City, for he moved to American club Portland Timbers in March 1980. He is currently assistant to Oldham manager Joe Royle.

Big Joe Corrigan was well established in goal and playing on top form—and in the next 12 months he was certainly going to need to have all his wits about him as the pressure built up. Speedy full-back Ray Ranson, who had joined the club as an apprentice from St Helens, was a key part of the defence. The fluent Tommy Caton and dependable Tommy Booth, two great City stalwarts, were still doing their part. But it was the new faces that arrived during the season that surprised the City supporters. City had looked to Europe for talent and signed Polish international Kazimeirz Deyna from Liega, Warsaw, for £120,000. Deyna was the former skipper of Poland during the World Cup which was played in Argentina. Yet although he showed a lot of flair, the 30-year-old Pole never quite had the impact that Tony Book had been hoping for.

In July 1979 manager Allison went to a board meeting to tell the directors he wanted to buy an unknown midfielder called Steve Mackenzie from Crystal Palace. Mackenzie, a dark-haired, likeable youngster, was certainly getting rave reviews. Allison believed he was going to be a great star of the future. He had already made inquiries and had been given a fee from Palace which he thought reasonable considering the extraordinary promise Mackenzie was showing. Allison felt in every sense of the word that he was an investment for the future. When one of the City directors asked how much this youngster was going to cost the club, Allison replied, 'Two hundred and fifty.' The director smiled. 'Well, that sounds a damn good deal at £250.' But Allison countered genially, 'No, you misunderstood me. He will cost us £250,000.' Nonetheless, chairman Swales and his men decided to go along with Allison and Mackenzie was duly brought to Maine Road.

Another foreign player to arrive was the big Yugoslav Dragoslav Stepanovic, from the German club Wormatia Worms. The big defender was another who failed to make the grade in the new season, and after a dozen games he was dropped. On 2 June, before that season, City also signed striker Bobby Shinton from Wrexham for £375,000. Allison maintains he was not happy with the signing and that again it was a player Tony Book and the City board had been chasing before he had returned to Maine Road. 'I heard Tony talking about signing him when I had only been back at the club for a few days. I was not happy because I didn't think he had good positional sense.'

Then a few weeks later, City splashed out £750,000 for Preston North End's exciting striker Michael Robinson. Again, Allison tells me, the transfer was not set up by him. Nonetheless, the fans thought that this was another new hope for the future.

So City set off bravely into a new season. Along with players already mentioned, there was the indefatigable Paul Power, along with tenacious Tony Henry and Dave Bennett. It was to prove a disappointing season with more big money being splashed out for players. City struggled in the League and went crashing out of the FA Cup at little Halifax Town, who won by the only goal of the tie. City were already out of the League Cup, having lost in a third round replay at Sunderland 1-0. But despite everything chairman Peter Swales and his board were still coming up with big money to back the return of Allison. In January of 1980 the dependable Dennis Tueart was brought back from New York Cosmos for £150,000 and then in early March, City splashed out a massive £1,250,000 for striker Ken Reeves of Norwich City. Allison maintains, 'He wasn't my particular choice, but the chairman had seen him playing for Young England and was tremendously impressed. I said that if he thought he was such a great a player, then go ahead and sign him. So we did. But it was not my idea to sign him in the first place.'

The start of the 1980-81 season was disastrous for Allison and Book. The young City team showed genuine flashes of exceptional promise. Nobody was denying that there was plenty of talent there but the trouble lay with the teamwork. The players just hadn't got a true understanding of one another. They couldn't fit into a winning football unit.

The City side played in fits and starts and the results were appalling. They didn't win any of the first 11 League fixtures, losing seven, and were sitting firmly and sadly at the foot of the First Division table. After a 3-1 defeat at West Brom it was all over. The City board met two days later and the decision was taken to fire both Allison and Book, although Book was re-appointed as coach at a later date.

It was a sad state of affairs because Allison had assembled a side of mainly young players who excited a lot of people, not least the great Nottingham Forest manager Brian Clough. After City had lost 3-2 at the City ground, Clough had said, 'Given time, this City side can be a good one. They have got some very exciting young players.' But it was not to be. Book was philosophical, but maintains, 'Malcolm meant well, but he tried to do too much far too quickly. He got rid of some good experienced players we should have kept for the time being.'

Peter Gardner, top sports reporter for over 20 years, was closer to what happened in that period than anybody other than the participants themselves. 'Chairman Peter Swales brought Allison back because he thought he would be the man to give City the power to really challenge United at that time. Under Book they had been twice in the top eight of the First Division and won the League Cup in 1976. Then in 1977 they were runners-up in the championship race and fourth a year after. That was good going by any standard.

'Swales was utterly ambitious to make City the very best. Remember that the gates were averaging close to 40,000. But Malcolm was being pushed all the time by the board. The directors were anxious for success as quickly as possible, but in the end Allison let too many good players go too quickly and the youngsters were not quite ready for the challenge. I was sorry because Allison, for my money, was the finest coach in the game at that time. No one could match him. Yet because of all the pressure he just took too much on, and was never given a real chance.'

So Allison left the scene. But let no one forget what a prodigious talent he had. He was a magical figure and he made City so exciting.

CHAPTER THIRTEEN

SO ALLISON DEPARTED for a second time. Book also went, although he was to return at a later date to the club he loved and couldn't live without.

Once again the figures scurried from their cars and up the steps to the entrance of Manchester City Football Club. Another board meeting was called to decide who was to be the new manager of the club. Once again Swales sat at the top of the large table as his fellow directors listened to his plans. They nodded in agreement. It was to be John Bond, the current manager of Norwich. But it was to be an acrimonious situation for City this time. The Norwich chairman, Sir Arthur South, was livid at his manager being poached from under his nose. There were harsh words and the Norwich supremo warned Bond, 'You are making the biggest mistake of your life. You will live to regret the day you left this club.'

Although at that time Bond believed those were only empty words, they were to haunt him, for the prophecy was painfully true. Bond does rue the day he took the Swales offer, yet he recalls the moment Swales approached him and asked him if he would be interested in coming to Manchester City. 'He couldn't have come at a better moment,' says Bond. 'I desperately wanted to be a manager of a really big club as much as I enjoyed it at Norwich City. I kept seeing the big boys coming to Carrow Road, the likes of Manchester United and City, Liverpool and Leeds United. I loved the big-time atmosphere that surrounded clubs like that. I wanted a part of that sort of action. It was a natural thing for a young ambitious manager. So when Swales made his move I was more than ready to take a chance and have a go at it.'

But Bond had enjoyed six and a half 'magnificently happy years', as he puts it, with Norwich. He had been exceptionally successful and the club had appreciated his worth to them and had rewarded him royally. Bond had a massive contract which still had seven and a half years to run. Moreover, Bond reveals today, 'Sir Arthur had promised me I would be given the position as general manager of Norwich City when I felt I had had enough as team manager. He also assured me that he and the rest of the directors fully intended to see me join the board eventually. It was a dream set-up.' Yet when anyone else in the cut-throat game of professional football would have jumped at it, Bond simply turned his back and walked away.

But there was an early warning for Bond that all was not what it seemed at Manchester City, for on arriving on his first day at the club he was invited by Swales to attend a board meeting. As the business unfolded, Bond suddenly realised he was still not officially manager of the club. 'Chairman Peter Swales asked the directors if they would like to indicate by a show of hands that I should be appointed manager of the club,' reveals Bond. 'But a director, Ian Niven, said, "I have never met the manager who could replace Malcolm Allison. But if the chairman wants you then I will go along with that."'

A lot of people must have wondered if it was 007 instead of John Bond who had arrived at Maine Road in the 1980-81 season. Bond not only transformed City's position as relegation possibilities, he brought the whole vibrant club to life. There was a touch of the swagger about the place that recalled the happy days of Mercer and Allison. Not only that, Bond started to turn the team into one that played with dash and colour. There was an air of excitement when a Bond team took the pitch. It didn't always work out, they didn't always win. But they played with a cockiness that the fans loved. At last City seemed to be on the way to winning something big with a man like John Bond in command. His backroom staff of ex-City player John Benson, who was Bond's number two, and first-team coach John Sainty also settled in well. They were popular and liked a lot of fun.

Yet when the confident and bluff Bond sat down and assessed the task before him, even he must have felt a slight shudder of apprehension in October of that season. City's humiliating record showed that they hadn't won a single game so far and had only four points from 11 games. 'I sat there in the manager's office,' says Bond, 'and recalled Allison's parting remark as he left when he said, "We were just about to take off." In fact, the team was going nowhere. There was no real plan and little spirit. I just had to change things right away. They were utterly negative and it had to be altered drastically to save our First Division lives. I remember watching them in action for the first time and I saw them pass the ball 20 times yet never get out of their own half. I had to release them from their shackles.'

Bond's first signing certainly raised a few eyebrows. He was Tom Hutchison, from Coventry City, who was 33 years old. Hutchison had not only exceptional skill but a fierce will to win that rubbed off on the rest of the playing staff. 'I had always fancied signing him when I was at Norwich,' says Bond. 'My son Kevin was playing out in Seattle. I went out to watch Kevin and Hutchison was playing. He simply tore the opposition to shreds. He has such a magnificent attitude to the game and I knew I had to sign him. He is just a great player to have in your club. When I was at City, Kevin rang me and said Hutchison had returned to this country. I rang him and he drove up. He wasn't keen to sign because he had heard City didn't pay good money. But I offered him top cash and he signed there and then. I knew I was already on the way to getting the game right on the pitch and the spirit right in the dressing-room with Tom on the staff. We never looked back after that.'

Hutchison was joined by another Coventry man, Bobby McDonald, a tough defender who also didn't like losing one little bit. Gerry Gow was bought in from Bristol City. 'They were all good signings and I gave them top contracts and they repaid me by their devotion to getting things on a winning footing,' says Bond. 'They brought the best out of the younger players like Nicky Reid, Ray Ranson and Tommy Caton. It just took off from there and the fans loved it.' Yet in Bond's first game in charge and before the three new players were signed City slumped to a 1-0 defeat by Birmingham City at Maine Road in front of 30,041 fans. The majority of those supporters must have shuffled homewards, dispirited and utterly convinced Bond would have to wave a magic wand to transform their team. Well, he did. In his own words, 'After that defeat by Birmingham, we simply roared away. It was a marvellous time.' Bond was named manager of the month twice in succession.

Bond had learned his football at West Ham United under the ideal management of Ron Greenwood, who was renowned for the excellent quality of his teams. The same polish was exhibited now at City. Bond's side had been transformed from a struggling team into an attacking outfit capable of turning anybody over. Bond was relishing the challenge. A high point came in February when City licked old enemy United in front of a crowd of 50,000 fans at Maine Road, thanks to a Steve Mackenzie goal. City's First Division future was already secure. Surely that in itself was enough for Bond. Not a bit of it.

City were to have tremendous runs in both the League Cup and the FA Cup. Turning first to the League Cup performances, it has to be remembered that City stormed to the semi-final of the competition without the three new players who had been brought in during the autumn and who were already cup-tied. In the second round Stoke were sent crashing out 4-1 on aggregate and then there followed a 2-1 win at Luton. In round four, Dennis Tueart scored four of City's goals in the 5-1 trouncing of Notts County. West Brom were City's next victims losing 2-1, and Dave Bennett had scored in every round. So next City faced mighty Liverpool in the two-leg semi-final. If any of their fans expected City to be overawed by the Merseyside giants they were happily mistaken. City gave them a terrific battle at Maine Road and although Liverpool won 1-0, the referee disallowed a headed goal by Kevin Reeves. 'It looked a perfect goal,' recalls Bond. 'The referee said he had disallowed it, as it was illegal jumping, but even Liverpool looked surprised at his decision. That goal would have made a vital difference.' Bond was right—they performed brilliantly at Anfield for a 1-1 draw, with Reeves getting the goal. It was a stunning show from a squad of players branded a bunch of 'nervous failures' before Bond took them by the scruff of the neck and made them realise just what can be achieved when you can truly believe in yourself.

Next was the FA Cup, and Bond says, 'It was such an exciting time. You could hardly credit how things had turned around in such a short time. There was so much confidence in the team—even a little cockiness. But everyone was really enjoying the football and that means so much in the professional game. The sky's the limit if you are in that sort of mood.'

Amazingly, City drew Malcolm Allison's Crystal Palace in the third round of the FA Cup at Maine Road. Here was a sweet victory for Bond as City crushed Palace 4-0 with goals from Kevin Reeves (2), Paul Power and Ian Bowyer.

In the fourth round of the FA Cup and by sheer irony, City drew Bond's old club Norwich at Maine Road and hammered them 6-0 with goals flowing from Bobby McDonald, Kevin Reeves, Steve Mackenzie, Paul Power, Gerry Gow and Dave Bennett. A crowd of 38,919 watched the soccer slaughter.

The fifth round called for a tough trip to Peterborough where City came through a dodgy 90 minutes with a 1-0 win, thanks to a goal by Tommy Booth. The next round was tough—a trip to Goodison to play Everton. It was a real battle but goals from Paul Power and Gerry Gow brought them a 2-2 draw and a replay at Maine Road. There was a crowd of 52,532 for the second meeting which City won convincingly 3-1 with goals from Bobby McDonald (2) and Paul Power. City were now in the semi-final of the FA Cup.

A lot of the Blues fans had to pinch themselves. Could it really be that they were now one match from Wembley? Well, if they could beat Ipswich Town they certainly would be. It was a stiff one, for manager Bobby Robson had assembled a classy Ipswich side, but there was a twofold reason Bond particularly wanted to win this one. Robson had always seemed to have the Indian sign on Bond and it irritated the new City boss. 'Somehow, he always seemed to be able to put one over on us when I was at Norwich. I didn't like the way he smirked about his success. This was the big one and I felt this was going to be the big breakthrough in my managerial career.' Yet their clash gave Bond some heart-stopping moments. The 46,537 crowd were on the edges of their seats, especially City's fans. It looked to be going Ipswich's way in a blindingly white-hot semi-final struggle.

Bond is sportingly frank in his appraisal of that desperate clash for the right to stride out at Wembley. As the battle raged, he recalls feeling Ipswich had the opportunity to finish off his fighting men. 'They certainly had three or four chances to win it,' remembers Bond. 'But the supporters on that afternoon were fantastic to Manchester City. They kept roaring and waving and lifted the lads. When it went into extra time and our boys started to show their strength and resilience, I suddenly felt it was going to be our day. It was a tremendous feeling.' As the tension of the deadlock reached unbearable proportions, several of the City players' wives left their seats in the stands and just walked within the confines of the stadium beyond the sight of the pitch, praying the Blues would make it.

In the second period of extra time, City won a free kick on the edge of the Ipswich box. Paul Power elected to take it. The stadium was hushed. Power swung his trusty left foot to send the ball circling over the Ipswich defensive wall. In his entire career he has never struck a sweeter blow. The ball flew a few inches inside the far upright and rippled down the back of the net with the Ipswich players staring in horror. A mammoth roar rang out from the thousands of throats of the City supporters and every Blues supporter leapt to his feet to acclaim the goal that surely would take City to Wembley. It did. It was the decisive killer-blow that put Robson's men on the canvas. They never regained their feet before the final whistle.

The Villa Park was ablaze with City's sky-blue scarves and banners. Fans, players, everyone connected with the club, were dancing with jubilation. Yet Bond recalls, 'As the moment came when we knew we had reached Wembley against all the odds, in a natural reaction in victory I seized the chairman in a hug of celebration. Swales never reacted. The moment of pure football triumph just didn't mean anything to him. He just didn't show the reaction that thousands of supporters were showing—that this was an incredible day of success for all of us. No, he couldn't. Because I'm certain all he wants is the chance to control the club—not the basic thrill of participation in a football club that you get when it wins.'

So Bond's incredible bandwagon rumbled on to Wembley and the excitement his bold style of soccer had created had the fans believing anything was possible now. Not even the threat of star-studded Tottenham Hotspur, who were waiting for them in the final, scared them now. City were going for it with a vengeance.

Bond approached the clash with glittering Tottenham Hotspur with zest and confidence. 'Okay, they looked a formidable outfit on paper,' recalls the ex-City chief, 'but I don't think there was one member of our squad who did not believe we could beat them. Confidence was as high as Mount Everest.' Bond decided upon his final line-up: Joe Corrigan, with Ray Ranson, Bobby McDonald, Nicky Reid, Paul Power, Tommy Caton, Bennett, Gow, Mackenzie, Hutchison, Kevin Reeves, with Tony Henry as substitute.

When ranged against this Tottenham side packed with star names, City's chances looked pretty thin if you were neutral; Aleksic, Chris

106

Hughton, Paul Miller, Graham Roberts, Steve Perryman, Ricky Villa, Brooke, Ossie Ardiles, Steve Archibald, Galvin, Hoddle, Crooks. The referee was Keith Hackett of Sheffield.

City were utterly relaxed as they changed for the match all players dream of being involved in. Bond and John Benson kept up a lot of banter but quickly realised their squad didn't need relaxing. There was no sign of nerves. 'We really thought we would win the game,' says Bond. 'But I have always gone along with Tommy Docherty's theory—if your name is on the Cup, then you will win it. Quite simply, ours wasn't and that's why we didn't. But I have not been more proud of any team I have managed or played in than I was in those lads who fought it out that day. They deserved a better fate.'

City's performance was exhilarating. After 30 minutes they had silenced Tottenham's screaming hordes by surging into a shock lead— and it was Hutchison, the oldest player on the field, who got it. Bond's faith in the long-legged veteran Scot paid off in a big way. Following a free kick, Ray Ranson crossed into the box and Hutchison threw himself like a spear to connect for a header that flew unerringly past the helpless Aleksic. Wembley was a sea of white and blue at one end as the City fans went mad.

Spurs tried desperately to strike back. But the accolade to Bond's battling side was that they held firm. It was difficult to recall that Bond had been brought to Manchester City back in October with the objective of saving the team from relegation. Yet now they could be on their way to lifting the FA Cup.

How desperately close they came to pulling off a sensational victory in that original final. Steve Mackenzie, who was confirming in attacking fashion Allison's prophecy that he would be one of the great players of the future, was cruelly denied a second City goal. He tricked his way into the Spurs box, even got past goalkeeper Aleksic. But with an open goal beckoning, the awkward angle of his scoring chance saw him screw the ball against the outside of the post and it went rolling on the wrong side. Fate was against them. But City were still only a breathless gasp away from lifting the FA Cup in that agonising moment.

With only ten slim minutes left, heartbreak followed as fate so cruelly turned on hero Hutchison. Glen Hoddle cracked a centre into the City box following a free kick. In trying to clear it, the hard-working Hutchison only half hit the ball and deflected it past the wrong-footed Joe Corrigan into the net. Hutchison sank to his knees in misery. Nothing could relieve his sickening disappointment of that moment. But illustrating the nerve and spirit Bond had already built, 'keeper Corrigan quickly gave him a commiserating smack on his back, clearly saying, 'Forget it. We are still in this battle.' So, for the first time since Wembley had become the home of FA Cup finals, there was to be a replay—at night, midweek.

After all Bond had achieved, he now expected a sense of excitement and jubilation in his City camp. True, it was disappointing to be pipped at the post by Spurs, but he was surely right to feel immense pride in that extraordinary performance. However, the reaction of the City board appalled him on that golden Wembley performance. Says Bond with a philosophical shrug, 'It was fate that we weren't to win that final. It was sickening after the way the players had battled, outwitted and often outplayed a team like Spurs. But that's football. That's the way it goes in the game. You have to accept that sometimes the breaks go against you. I could accept all that.' What Bond couldn't stomach was the lack of reaction by the City board to the full-blooded performance his team had produced in that great Wembley display against a team most of the football world expected would steamroller Manchester City into the ground. 'There wasn't an ounce of excitement in the City party at what that side had achieved,' says John. 'While the fans were desperately disappointed at the way Spurs had come back to grab a draw by a fluke goal, they were thrilled by the team's display. But not the City board. We might have lost from their reaction.' But a determined Bond refused to dwell on their bitter disappointment. He rallied his troops. 'We can do it again and this time beat them.' So Bond primed his men for the second battle. If the world of football thought the original final had been a fluke display by a City side hyped up by Bond, they were to be kept on the edge of their seats in the midweek replay by one of the most exciting Cup final games ever witnessed at Wembley.

City carried the battle to Tottenham with a vengeance that surprised Birkenshaw's camp. Ricky Villa, that marauding Argentinian, squirmed through to give Spurs the lead. But Steve Mackenzie produced one of the greatest strikes ever seen in a Wembley final to send the blistering volley into the net from the edge of the box. It was like a never-say-die boxer who had been down on the canvas only to topple his opponent for the count immediately afterwards. That extraordinary volley of power and accuracy kept the huge band of City faithful delirious with delight. It looked as if all the struggle and determination this City side had showed through this quite momentous season was to be crowned in triumph.

When Bennett was fouled, Kevin Reeves stepped up to rifle home the spot kick. Surely City, battling, pushing and creating classy sweeps of soccer, were on their way to a trophy they deserved if only for their sheer guts. It was not to be. In a flurry of attacks, first Garth Crooks scrambled the ball past Corrigan and the game was level. Then the final blow. In great finals so tensely balanced, stirring matches of the highest magnitude, there so often appears a player with a moment of sheer magic to swing it his side's way. On this occasion, and to City's chagrin, it was Ricky Villa. The ball-juggling Argentinian produced the greatest moment of his football career when he stormed through City's pressurised defence and, after gliding into the box, slipped the winning goal past a helpless goalkeeper Joe Corrigan.

The heartbreak for City was not that they had lost a Cup final but that they had had the misfortune to meet a team with a player of Villa's world class who could suddenly grab glory out of thin air. Bond had built a team virtually out of nothing and made them look like world beaters, only for their moment of soccer history to be destroyed by one flash of genius. Quite rightly, everyone rose to acknowledge the solo genius of Villa. It was a night of tears for City. Yet Bond's pride in that team and what it achieved is enormous. He will never forget it. He told me, 'I could not have had more from a squad of players than I had from those guys. They were superb. But once again, the reaction from the City board was pathetic. They just didn't react or acknowledge what had been achieved. Only a few months earlier we were fighting relegation. Now the club was safe and had reached Wembley. They just didn't want to know.'

Looking back, Bond now truly believes he should have taken a shock decision after that heartbreaking Wembley replay. 'On reflection, I can see that I should have handed in my resignation,' says Bond. But it would not have been because of the defeat. Bond was as proud of his men and their performance in defeat as he would have been had they won. 'I should have resigned because I had already realised City were never going to be a big club as long as they had so many small-minded people running it at the top. I certainly came very close to quitting when we were in the Royal Garden Hotel. We were having dinner. There was a feeling of nastiness in the company that I didn't like. It became obvious to me, listening to people talking then, that this club couldn't handle either success or failure. At Norwich we had lost big matches but still had a big night out and enjoyed ourselves. But that night with City's people I wasn't happy at all. It all seemed to be so small and so petty.'

Bond somehow managed to bottle up his frustration and decided to get on with the job. Maybe there would be a change in outlook, he reasoned. At the beginning of the next season, 1981-82, he was determined to make the City board think big.

He had been enormously impressed by the tremendous following of the City fans throughout their dramatic run to Wembley and during the two terrific battles they had fought in the famous stadium. The City boss felt the club should reward those supporters and himself with enough money to buy a really crack player who could start a realistic charge for the championship. The player Bond wanted was Nottingham Forest and England striker Trevor Francis. Swales agreed it could be done. But even during the negotiations over the signing of the superstar there was to be rancour and bitterness. Bond was delighted to be getting Francis, who had the class to give City the flair and scoring power a top First Division side needed. The deal was partially financed by selling Steve Mackenzie to West Brom for £450,000—a move that didn't please many of the City faithful. Bond describes the way the transfer went. 'I drove Swales down to Derby where I was to meet Trevor and settle the transfer. I met him along with his agent and four other people who were involved. I then walked out after being told the deal would go through. It was arranged for Trevor to see a Harley Street specialist. But when Swales and I were driving back the chairman said to me, "The deal won't be going through." I don't know why he said that. But I immediately replied, "If the deal doesn't go through then I shall resign." Both Swales and John Benson knew that I was definitely going to quit if the transfer wasn't completed. Eventually, they persuaded me to wait and see what was going to happen. But later the deal did go through. I never had anything to do with the actual transfer. I was just there to talk to Trevor. Nothing more. The rest was handled by the chairman.'

So once again it was the same old story. The manager did not do the wheeling and dealing. That was handled by Swales. Francis made an immediate impact. He scored twice on his debut in the 3-1 win at Stoke City in the third match of the season. Boyer scored the other goal. Bond was delighted. 'I told Francis that he was going to play a major role in helping us win the championship very soon,' says Bond.

Bond strengthened his squad further by signing Northern Ireland international Martin O'Neill from his old club Norwich City, for £275,000, and his son Kevin from Seattle Sounders (£350,000). Then he re-signed Asa Hartford from Everton for £375,000. City were now a side to be reckoned with. In little over a year Bond had transformed a City side that seemed all set for the Second Division into a championship-chasing outfit. Joe Corrigan was proving a great goalkeeper in the making. Full-back Ray Ranson was at his peak. Nick Reid was in tigerish form and Bond's son Kevin, along with the exciting Tommy Caton, added flair to the scene. Dennis Tueart was scoring some mouth-watering goals and Paul Power was as cool and quick a defender as you could find in the First Division. Steve Kinsey looked a flying winger of considerable prospect and Scottish international Asa Hartford was proving inspirational in his powerful midfield role. Bond had assembled a lot of class. Francis fitted into the outfit perfectly.

City started strongly and by Christmas they really showed how far they had come when they went to Anfield and beat Liverpool 3-1. Hartford gave them a lead with a fine piece of opportunism and Kevin Bond cracked in a penalty for the second. Although Ronnie Whelan pulled one back for Liverpool, Reeves snapped up City's third and City now looked championship material. In the next game they licked Wolves 2-1 thanks to goals from Hartford and Francis. They were now top of the First Division. Yet the second half of the season was a let-down after their magnificent charge over the first part of the programme. City won only three of their last 17 games and finished tenth.

Yet despite the disappointment of their championship hopes fading in that season, Bond was optimistic about the future. 'I felt we had the nucleus there in place. We just needed one or two more players. When Liverpool or Manchester United realised they hadn't quite the strength their squad needed, then the board always made sure there was the opportunity to do it.' But far from being allowed to strengthen his hand, Bond was shattered when chairman Peter Swales suddenly announced they were going to sell their best player—Trevor Francis. Crack Italian side Sampdoria had come in for him and that was that. Francis was gone at the end of the season. Bond reflects bitterly, 'It was the end of any championship hopes for City when the decision was made to sell Trevor. I felt if we had kept him and bought just one or two more top-flight players, then we would have won the title.

'It was the old, old story. City desperately needed the money once again. At that point, in my opinion, if we had had the solid support from the City board, we could have built a truly great side— ready to compete with the very best. But it was all thrown away when we had to sell Francis.'

Before the start of the next season, Bond had a great chance to move into Continental football. He was offered the lucrative job of becoming manager of Portuguese giants Benfica. He was also told he could take his number two, John Benson, with him. 'It was a great temptation,' says Bond. But after much soul searching they both decided to turn down the offer. They felt maybe it would still come right at City.

The new season saw David Cross arrive from West Ham, for £135,000, in the role of striker. Graham Baker was also signed from Southampton, for £225,000. Cross scored on his début at Norwich after only three minutes of the new campaign, making it the quickest goal in the League on that Saturday. In the third game of the season at home to Watford, goalkeeper Joe Corrigan had to be helped off the pitch early in the game after dislocating his shoulder. Bobby McDonald took over in goal and performed heroically to keep a clean sheet. City won the game 1-0 through a Dennis Tueart goal. Yet although City started that season brightly, winning four of their first five games, they couldn't find that vital consistency for a push for the championship. But Bond insists, 'The failure to strengthen the team after the previous season had been a big mistake. We had not brought in players of a high enough quality needed to make us a top team.'

The end of the road as far as a disconsolate John Bond was concerned came after City were drawn at Brighton in the fourth round of the FA Cup after having beaten Sunderland 2-1 in a third round replay at Maine Road. This tie at Brighton was one of those nasty ones all managers of a big club fear. It had all the makings of a giant-killing. Sure enough, with the Brighton fans all wound up and roaring on their side on the sloping pitch, the Brighton players were ready for their big day. They played out of their skins.

Brighton hit the sort of form that was good enough to upset the biggest of clubs. It was a typical Cup-tie performance. Brighton won 4-0 and were to march all the way to the FA Cup final, ironically losing to Manchester United.

As far as Bond was concerned that was the end of the road for him. 'There was a row in the dressing-room and I realised that there were several players in the side who should have gone by now. I had wanted them replaced by really classy men but I hadn't been given the money to sign top-class performers and that was why we were struggling.' Bond drove back to London with a friend, feeling bitterly disappointed at the way things had worked out for him at Manchester City, after all his hopes on joining them from Norwich. Then when the car stopped at some traffic lights in Brighton, some City fans saw him. 'There were four of them and they recognised me,' says Bond. 'Their behaviour was vile. The abuse was unbelievable and one of them spat at the car. As we drove on I said to my friend, "That's it. I shall resign on Monday." Bond still hesitated, though, as his close friends tried to persuade him to soldier on. 'But on the Thursday I saw the chairman Peter Swales and told him I wished to resign. He didn't try to dissuade me.'

Bond was never to have the same tremendous impact at another club as he had at Manchester City. He drifted to clubs such as Burnley, Birmingham City, Swansea and Shrewsbury Town. That inspirational spark didn't flash any more. Bond and his amiable aide, John Benson, did a miraculous job in transforming things at Maine Road. It is a pity they are not still a management pair in the game. Football is the poorer for their absence.

CHAPTER FOURTEEN

AS JOHN BOND turned his back defiantly on Maine Road and strode away to seek his soccer fortune elsewhere, the City board found themselves once again in a quandary. Bond insists it was not because of the shock 4-0 FA Cup defeat at Brighton that he left, but because he felt the board would not give him the backing in the transfer market he desperately needed to build up a side capable of winning trophies. His assistant John Benson agreed. 'Time and again he was turned down by the board when he wanted to bring in certain players,' says Benson. 'It finally got him down. He felt he was not being allowed to manage the team and that his authority was being undermined. He had some wonderful ideas for strengthening the team by selling some players and buying better replacements. But he was always thwarted. It got him down and he had had enough.'

When Bond resigned in February 1983, the board's biggest problem was whether to promote Benson rather than bring in a new man. Benson had certainly got the right pedigree. He had been brought up in neighbouring Stockport as a youngster and had played for Manchester City in the early '60s for two seasons. He made over 40 appearances before being transferred to Torquay United in 1964 for £5,000. He made over 200 appearances for the seaside club before moving to Bournemouth where he linked up for the first time with John Bond. After being transferred to Exeter City, Benson then moved to Norwich where Bond was then manager. Bond eventually appointed him as a player-coach. When Bond moved to Maine Road in 1980 he surprised a lot of people in football by taking Benson with him from Norwich as his deputy manager when several other people appeared more likely candidates. Benson had a rich sense of humour and was popular in the dressing-room with the players.

The City board duly decided Benson could steer them through the rest of the season. If he did well, they felt they might give him a good contract. If not, then they could cast around for a new manager in the meantime. But although he took the job, Benson maintains he never really wanted it. 'I realise with hindsight that I should have followed my first impulse and turned the job down,' says Benson reflectively. 'The club was going downhill in everybody's opinion and there was no money for players. Yet I took the job because I genuinely felt for City. Look at it this way. Twenty years earlier I achieved my wildest dreams when I played for the club as a young- ster. As a kid, I had been mad about the place. Indeed, in one sense the City board could not have handed the job to a man with a greater love for Manchester City and all the club stood for in the world of football.'

In March, City lost the services of the indestructible Joe Corrigan, a goalkeeper who had battled to the very top of his profession. Despite early setbacks in his career and a point where a small band of supporters turned on him, which almost caused him to quit Maine Road, the defiant, big-hearted Corrigan fought to the top. He forged a reputation to be set alongside the great City 'keepers of the past like the mighty Frank Swift and Bert Trautmann. It had been the constant encouragement of people like Trautmann that kept Corrigan battling on. Although the sparks often flew between them at times of friction, coach Malcolm Allison played a major role in big Joe getting his weight down to enable him to produce his most spectacular goalkeeping performances. But in March 1983 Corrigan was given a transfer to play in the American League with Seattle Sounders. It was a generous move by the City board to release him. For it gave Joe the chance of earning a nice bit of money which was no more than he deserved after his long and loyal service at Maine Road. City had a highly capable replacement from the reserves in the young Alex Williams, who was eager for a prolonged run in the senior side.

In April striker David Cross also left for American football and joined Vancouver Whitecaps. 'I needed a replacement,' says Benson. 'I wasn't happy seeing him go but the board decided the transfer was right for the club. I asked to be allowed to buy Jimmy Quinn, a very capable goal-getter with Stockport County. The fee would have been £50,000 and County were desperate for money. They would have let City have him for a small deposit. But again the board couldn't see their way to buying him. I realised then that they had only put me in the job because they couldn't really afford to bring in someone from the outside. I realised that they should have hung on to John Bond and kept us together. The results just kept going against us, yet I felt if we could have bought Quinn and maybe one more quality player, we would have been safe in the First Division.'

But, yet again, the City ship was heading for the First Division relegation rocks. It was once more a battle to save it from sinking back into the Second Division. Ironically, on the penultimate League game of the season, City had to travel back to Brighton, scene of their humiliating FA Cup defeat back in January. Thanks to a goal by the razor-sharp Kevin Reeves, City won 1-0. Their First Division security demanded that they now must not lose to fellow strugglers Luton Town in the very last match of the season at Maine Road.

That victory at Brighton was a boost to Benson's morale. But when he picked up a Sunday newspaper the next day and glanced at the headlines his spirits took an immediate nosedive. He read that Jackie Charlton had been interviewed by City directors with a view to possibly being the new manager. 'That was the thing that hurt most of all,' says Benson. 'Surely they could have left any move for a new manager until we were safe rather than risk rocking the boat at such a delicate moment.'

The game with Luton will still be etched on the memory of every City fan who saw it. Yet again it seemed that the gypsy's curse had struck. City pressed constantly, with the huge 42,000 crowd roaring them on. Luton had some desperate moments but, with only minutes remaining, they seemed determined to hang on. No one was bothered as long as City took their life-saving point from the game, for then First Division football was assured at Maine Road the next season. Then disaster struck.

With only four minutes to go, Luton broke out in their only threatening move of that second half. The ball ran to substitute Antic, who hammered it past the despairing goalkeeper Williams who just failed to grasp the ball by inches. The Luton fans went absolutely crazy. City's followers were thunderstruck. It was the cruellest of blows, for City had done more than enough to have won this most critical of games quite handsomely. As the final whistle blew, Luton manager David Pleat came bursting on to the pitch in a dance of triumph. He dashed from one player to another, seizing them in a victory hug. Luton's bench was leaping about in ecstasy. Their jubilant celebrations only served to contrast starkly with the leaden misery of the City camp and their followers. In the long years of covering games at Maine Road, I cannot recall scenes of such bitter disappointment and utter dismay. Certainly, no one was more shattered by this blow than chairman Peter Swales. Despite all the blows that befell the City team during his time in the chair, he had always been able to put on a brave face and insist they would 'bounce back'. This blow shook him to the core. When he finally managed to face the press long after the match, he was still struggling to come to terms with the disaster. Because disaster it was. No one had emphasised over the years how utterly important it was for City to remain in the First Division. Now, thanks to one shock goal, City were back in Division Two. It was too sick to contemplate.

Nonetheless, Swales had to put on a brave face, sit down with his fellow directors and come up with yet another manager. Benson departed with a heavy heart. 'I had feared this might happen if we didn't strengthen the team. It wasn't the Luton match that put us down . . . it was a lot earlier than that,' he maintains.

If ever chairman Peter Swales and his board seemed to have landed a truly great manager it was in the summer of 1983 when the huge frame of the genial Billy McNeill, MBE, strode through the front door of Maine Road. The big former Celtic and Scotland defender had a magnificent record both as a player and as a manager. His playing career was quite prodigious and crammed with honours. He had collected 23 winners' medals including a fabulous European Cup winners' medal after Celtic had triumphed in 1967. He had played in nine championship-winning teams and taken part in nine Scottish League Cup finals, being on the winning side on six occasions. He won 29 Scottish international caps and played over 800 games for Celtic. McNeill was awarded the MBE in 1974 and retired in the following year. After managing Aberdeen, he was appointed the team boss of Celtic to replace the legendary Jock Stein. He had an impressive five seasons there before Peter Swales persuaded him to go to Manchester City.

It was shrewd timing by Swales for McNeill was unhappy at the failure of the Celtic board to come up with an improved contract both he and the supporters felt he more than deserved. 'I was unhappy at the way things were going at Celtic at that time,' McNeill told me. 'I wasn't seeing eye to eye with them over the way things were to go in the future. So when Manchester City contacted me, I felt it would be the fresh challenge that I needed at that time. Nobody had to tell me what a great club Manchester City were. They had a marvellous past with hundreds of classy players passing through their doors. I really fancied the opportunity and the challenge. City was a kind of cavalier club with lots of style in their great days. So I thanked Peter Swales and his directors and said I would take it on.'

The fans were rubbing their hands in keen anticipation. At last the good days were going to roll again. Here was a man with class and character. It was going to be like the great Joe Mercer days all over again.

There was to be a Scottish alliance at City for that 1983-84 season, for there had been a flood of applicants for the job which McNeill had landed and one of them was Jimmy Frizzell, another Scot. Frizzell had played for Morton in the late '50s, before joining Oldham Athletic in 1960. He rattled in 57 goals in just over 300 matches. He was appointed manager in 1970 and did a quite extraordinary job in taking Athletic from the Fourth Division into the Second and almost into the First Division. Then in a move that totally shocked and stupefied the football world, Oldham dismissed him before the start of the 1982-83 season.

Frizzell was a popular figure on the Manchester football scene and was rumoured to have a great chance of landing the City job. He had been told by City that he was on the short list before going on holiday to Italy. 'I received a call in Italy from Peter Swales saying he was sorry to say that I hadn't got the job,' reveals Frizzell. 'But he told me, "Ring me when you get back as there may be something else in the pipeline."' When Frizzell got back to Manchester he contacted Swales and was told to meet him at the Bowden Hotel in Cheshire. 'When I walked into the room, there was Billy McNeill whom I didn't know well but obviously respected enormously,' says Frizzell. 'The question from both Billy and Swales was, would I take the job of assistant manager? I said I would be delighted. We met at lunchtime and I started work at Maine Road that same afternoon.'

It was bitterly ironic that Frizzell should be picked to join McNeill in the drive to get City back into the First Division, for it had been Frizzell who had played a major role in causing City to be relegated. 'I had been contacted a lot earlier by David Pleat, the Luton manager, who asked me to give him a complete breakdown on City's team and its possible weaknesses,' says Frizzell. 'He wanted my help in drawing up his strategy for the match. So I went along and watched City's games. I feel that I did manage to pinpoint the weaknesses in the City side—especially the defence. David Pleat was pleased at the result of it all when they won 1-0 to stay up. But I must admit that I felt bitterly sorry for City when they were relegated. I had always had a soft spot for Maine Road, like so many other people in football. But I was purely doing a job of work at the time.'

But as McNeill and Frizzell settled down to draw up their plans of strengthening their playing staff, the old bogey that had stumped so many previous managers appeared once again—the lack of finance to buy new players. Says McNeill, 'I had big plans to try to bring in some of the colourful players around at that time like Kevin Keegan, Peter Beardsley or Chris Waddle. They would have given the side such a shot in the arm and built up attendances in a big way. Most of all, I felt that it would demonstrate most clearly to our supporters that we really were trying to put City back in the big time.'

City's financial resources were stretched to the limit. McNeill was shocked at the lack of cash for the type of player he had been hoping to bring to Maine Road. 'I must be fair to the chairman Peter Swales,' McNeill told me. 'He had never promised me there would be a lot of money for transfers. But I didn't realise when I took the job that the club had such financial difficulties. Yet he was utterly frank and showed me the extent of the club's financial problems, which I considered extreme.' So in the words of McNeill's deputy Jimmy Frizzell the Scottish management pair had to pursue their new players 'on a shoestring'. They brought in Neil McNab from Brighton. This was an astute buy. McNab had been tipped for stardom when he was an exciting youngster with Spurs. His early displays at Maine Road quickly showed he would provide the vital midfield inspiration City so badly needed. Another Scot who arrived was Jim Tolmie, from the Belgian club Lokeren. He was followed by striker Derek Parlane, from Leeds United. But in December 1983, central defender Tommy Caton was sold to Arsenal for £500,000. That rather shattered City's supporters who held Caton in the highest regard. Then within weeks City splashed out £200,000 to bring sturdy Mick McCarthy from Barnsley. Centre-half McCarthy had been the centre of interest for a lot of other clubs at that time. It was to prove a profitable move for City, who were to sell McCarthy to Celtic for £500,000 four years later.

Everyone found Tommy Caton the most likeable of lads at Maine Road and he was extremely popular. I thoroughly enjoyed his company during interviews and he always had a happy grin and a laugh for everyone. He later left Arsenal for Oxford United and then Charlton Athletic. Like everyone else I was deeply saddened by his tragic death from a heart attack at the age of only 30 in 1993. Tommy will always be remembered for the inspiring displays and the joy he gave City fans in his days at Maine Road.

However, that season ended in disappointment, with City having to settle for fourth spot in the Second Division despite the success of the Derek Parlane-Jim Tolmie twin strike force. Between them they cracked home 34 League and Cup goals. 'It was a very frustrating time,' said McNeill. 'We were so close. But we just had to roll our sleeves up again and go for it the next season.'

McNeill and Frizzell strengthened the side during the 1984-85 season. They brought in striker Tony Cunningham from Sheffield Wednesday and Plymouth Argyle midfield man David Philips, who proved a big hit with the fans. He ended the season as joint leading scorer with 12 and many were real eye-catching efforts. There was the emergence from the reserve side of the impressive Andy May and tricky winger Paul Simpson who scored five very important goals in the last six matches of the season. This time City made it and the final match of the season in which they clinched the third spot to ensure promotion to the First Division was a real stunner. There was a whopping crowd of 47,285 at Maine Road to enjoy a 5-1 hammering of unfortunate Charlton Athletic. Two goals from David Philips and others from Andy May, Paul Simpson and Jim Melrose, who had been bought from Celtic in mid-season, completed the rout. City were back in the First Division.

An old friend returned to Maine Road during the close season with the signing of popular central defender Kenny Clements from Oldham. But the highlight of an otherwise rather grim season back in the First Division as City struggled for results was their performance in the much maligned new Full Members Cup. In the first tie City beat Leeds United 6-1, with Gordon Davies grabbing a hat-trick.

121

The other goals came from Baker, Paul Power and Mark Lillis who had been signed from Huddersfield and gave City some sterling service in his year at the club before being transferred to Derby County. Other victims as City marched to Wembley were Sheffield United, Sunderland (whom City beat on penalties) and then Hull City who were beaten 3-2 on aggregate in a two-legged semi-final. So the first final of the 'Mickey Mouse Cup', as it had been dubbed, drew a crowd of 68,000 at Wembley for the extraordinary shoot-out between City and Chelsea, on 23 March. The League insisted City had to play a derby match against United the day before. It ended in a 2-2 draw but cost City the services of Kenny Clements through injury. City lost the final but put up an amazing show. Quite near the end they were trailing 4-1 but battled back to finally lose a real thriller 5-4. David Speedie got a hat-trick for Chelsea. Lillis hit a couple, quicksilver Steve Kinsey got another and the fourth was a Chelsea own goal.

The 1985-86 season saw City managing to hang on to their First Division lives but the difficulties of being unable to buy quality players finally became too much for McNeill. By September of the following 1986-87 season McNeill had decided his future lay elsewhere. Yet with hindsight McNeill now believes he made a big mistake. 'I had been approached by Aston Villa, who made the job as manager at Villa Park sound extremely attractive. I just felt there was no future at City unless I could have the opportunity to bring in the sort of exciting players that were needed if the club was to have any real success. I wanted City to be a winner, up there with Manchester United and Liverpool, Leeds United and the rest. I felt utterly frustrated.' But when he told Jimmy Frizzell about his plans to go to Villa and asked for his view, Frizzell replied, 'I think you will be making a big mistake. I'm telling you, even though quite obviously I fancy having a crack as manager here if you go.'

But McNeill would not be persuaded. 'When I told the chairman Peter Swales that my mind was made up, he told me he was certain I would regret leaving. He said the Villa job was not what it looked. It wasn't long after moving to Villa Park that I realised immediately that I should not have left Maine Road. I should have bitten my lip and kept on with the job patiently. Maybe things might have worked out better had I soldiered on. I regret leaving City. But on the other hand, I have some wonderful memories of the people of Manchester and everyone at the Maine Road club.'

One of the strongest impressions McNeill has of his time at Maine Road was the 'quite staggering' work done by former City skipper Ken Barnes, who was chief scout during McNeill's management period. 'He performed absolute miracles in the face of incredible competition in the area from the likes of Manchester United, Liverpool and Everton. Ken had worked wonders over the years in the way he managed to land so many truly exciting lads,' says McNeill. 'City got the pick of the crop and just look at the way so many have passed through over the years. They were a wonderful bunch in the youth team and Ken deserves all the credit that's going. He had a remarkable knack of being able to spot true talent. He was brilliant in talking to the kids' parents and giving them the confidence to trust his judgment regarding the youngsters' future at Maine Road. He was rarely ever wrong in his judgment, and that was a remarkable ability. He was worth his weight in gold to the club for the way he kept the youngsters coming through.'

With the exit of McNeill to Villa, Swales decided that Frizzell would have to take over the reins on his own. 'The chairman came to me and asked, "Can you keep us up?" It was pretty obvious to anyone being asked that question that if you said no, you wouldn't get the job. But I honestly believed that I could. I told him I would need to buy some new players to strengthen the team to avoid relegation. I knew I was in for a very tough time indeed. Most of all I needed a top-class coach to work alongside me. I feared if it wasn't possible for one to be brought in that we would be struggling in our bid to avoid the drop. But I was determined to give it everything I had.'

Like all his predecessors, Frizzell was handicapped in not being able to bolster his squad with top-flight players. But he did well with the meagre resources available. He snapped up that remarkable striker Imre Varadi, from West Bromwich Albion, along with Republic of Ireland international Tony Grealish. It was a swap deal with Robert Hopkins—plus a small fee—going to the Hawthorns. The much-travelled Varadi was a one hundred per cent battler and the fans loved his fighting qualities. He linked up well with the exciting youngster Paul Moulden, who had just come into the first team after setting all sorts of scoring records in the City youth team. Moulden, though, was never quite able to repeat his extraordinary scoring knack at senior level. Frizzell maintains that he didn't get the right type of service. 'Paul wasn't a quick player,' says Frizzell.

'He lacked pace a little. But his team-mates always played the ball just that fraction too far in front of him. They should have played it right to his feet because he had wonderful control and could shoot so quickly and accurately. I tried to get the rest of the lads to realise this. But once they were out there in the thick of the play they still made the same mistake. Despite everything Paul was still doing a good job for us.'

Frizzell had a mixture of experience and youth. He had brought the skilful Peter Barnes back from Manchester United for his second spell at Maine Road, plus the experienced defender John Gidman, also from across the way at Old Trafford. The versatile defender Kenny Clements, who had played such a sterling role in City's defence during Tony Book's managerial years, had returned to Maine Road from Oldham. Perry Suckling, who had joined City from Coventry, was in goal, and some exciting youngsters were coming through like Ian Brightwell, Paul Simpson and David White. Frizzell felt the squad was just about strong enough for them to scrape above the First Division danger line—if they could keep getting goals. But a serious injury to Moulden in early January set the alarm bells ringing. It was pretty obvious City must bring in a top-class striker and quickly.

They already had one particular player in mind—Paul Stewart, a Manchester-born, bustling forward with Blackpool. A lot of other clubs were watching the form of the stocky Stewart and no one could quite make their minds up about him. 'We delayed for a number of reasons,' said Frizzell. 'Ken Barnes had a look at him, so did Tony Book and myself. He looked good, had a lot of pace, was very brave and could hit a ball with a lot of power. But he wasn't scoring that many goals. The argument was whether he could do it in the First Division. He was also going to be quite expensive as Blackpool were demanding £200,000, which was a heck of a lot of money at that time.' But City were still struggling and on 19 March Frizzell, after talks with the board, decided they must get their man. For Stewart it was a dream come true. He revealed he had always been a City man as a youngster. 'I am thrilled to be here and I believe I can do a good job for them,' he said. Stewart was to prove as good as his word—eventually.

But with 11 matches left, in which City had to fight for their First Division lives, would he be able to find his goal-scoring touch in the higher division quickly? It was a very tall order. City had had a terrible run since Moulden's injury, going 14 games without a win and picking up only six points. Stewart scored his first goal in a 4-2 defeat by Southampton, on 11 April. But although Moulden made a comeback and scored in that match, he had to be sidelined again because of a recurrence of the injury. Yet on 27 April there seemed real hope that City could still survive. They beat Arsenal 3-0 in exhilarating style and the attacking partnership of Stewart and Varadi looked razor sharp. Varadi scored a couple and Stewart got the other. Needing five points for survival over the last three matches, though, City slumped. They drew 0-0 at Everton and although a Varadi goal gave them a 1-0 victory over Nottingham Forest at Maine Road, a 2-0 defeat at West Ham saw them sliding back into the Second Division.

CHAPTER FIFTEEN

YET AGAIN it was time for a rethink at Maine Road, and once more, a manager was to appear. Originally, before the start of the 1987-88 season, there had been no suggestion made to Jimmy Frizzell that he would not still be in charge despite the disappointment of relegation. 'The chairman and myself were trying to bring in a top-class coach,' says Frizzell. 'I had always maintained such an addition was vital for the team's success and had felt we might have survived in the First Division the previous season if we had landed such a coach to help me. We had already tried to coax Mel Machin, from Norwich City, in the middle of the previous season. But he felt bound to honour his contract at Norwich. I had also tried to persuade Colin Harvey to see if he would take the job. But he maintained he was quite happy staying at Everton as first-team coach with manager Howard Kendall at Goodison.' So in the close season City went back to Norwich, from whom they had taken manager John Bond in 1980, for another attempt to persuade Machin to come to Maine Road. This time they got a willing response from quiet man Machin who was doing such a superb job in moulding unfashionable Norwich into one of the sweetest-looking footballing sides in England.

'The first time City approached me I was under contract,' says Machin. 'Maybe I am old fashioned, but I believed in loyalty to the club who had given the same to me. But when City approached me at the end of the season, I had an option clause in my contract and was perfectly entitled to take it up and discuss City's interest.'

Frizzell was happy to think Machin would be joining him. 'I had two meetings with Mel and I was very impressed by his ideas on the game. Finally we went to talk with Peter Swales at the chairman's house. It was at that meeting that Machin made it very clear that if he came he wanted to be in charge of all team affairs. In other words, that meant he wished to be the manager. In all fairness to the chairman, he was wonderful to me at that point. He just turned and asked me, "Well, what job do you want to have, Jimmy?" It wasn't as if he had said that Mel's desire to be manager meant I might have to look elsewhere for a job.' So Frizzell was made general manager. That was an extremely astute decision by the City chairman. During his long managership period at Oldham Athletic Frizzell had pulled off some very shrewd transfer deals, snapping up exciting players at knock-down prices and selling them a few years later for much larger fees. Frizzell was to repeat his knack time and again at City, working in tandem with whoever was the team manager.

Machin was delighted at his appointment. 'I felt ready for the chance to be the manager and a club of Manchester City's huge reputation in football represented a wonderful challenge,' says Machin. 'But I wasn't prepared for how weak the standard of football was from the playing staff.' That soon became manifest when he saw them in action during an end-of-season tour of West Africa. 'We lost against a very weak team out there,' says Machin. 'It was quite a shock for me to realise just how much improvement was needed in order to get the team anywhere near promotion standard.

'But looking on the brighter side, there were some very exciting youngsters coming through, with young England players like David White, Paul Lake, Steve Redmond and Ian Brightwell. The chief scout Ken Barnes had done a great job bringing youngsters like these through. But some of them had only played a handful of first-team games and, whilst it was encouraging to have them on hand, I certainly didn't want to have to rush them into action before they were ready. That would have ruined them. So I would have to get down to some wheeling and dealing in the transfer market.'

But yet again, the money was not available to buy the classy sort of players to give the team the zip and polish that would rocket it back into the First Division. Nonetheless, Machin got down to work. He brought in striker Trevor Morley from Northampton halfway through that 1987-88 season and with Paul Stewart now cracking in the goals, Machin completed a highly impressive first season with City ending up in a creditable ninth position in the Second Division. Stewart's tip-top shooting gallery performance was to win him rich pickings in the soccer big time. His goal-scoring feats had caught the eye of the big boys in the First Division and in June 1988 the telephone lines into Maine Road were humming with urgent inquiries.

Stewart had scored 28 goals in 52 League and Cup games. While it wasn't sensational, his all-round play was having a big impact up front for City. But the game that alerted everyone to his talent was City's 10-1 thrashing of Huddersfield Town in November 1987. (City's biggest score ever was when they knocked 11 past Lincoln City in March 1885.) Stewart, David White and Tony Adcock all hit hat-tricks, with the versatile Neil McNab getting the other goal. Adcock cracked in another hat-trick only three days later in a match against Plymouth Argyle in the Simod (formerly Full Members) Cup. But it was Stewart the big boys came chasing. It was here that Jimmy Frizzell, who had brought Stewart to Maine Road from Blackpool in the first place, showed his ability in astute dealing with the bidders to make sure City reaped a huge profit on the transfer. Tottenham Hotspur were first into the field with a bid around the £1 million mark. 'Then Graeme Souness, the Glasgow Rangers manager, came on and said he was very interested,' reveals Frizzell. 'But Paul went down to talk with Tottenham and he seemed very impressed after discussions with them. Then I had a call from Everton and I asked Paul if he wanted to talk to them. He did, and he went over to Goodison to discuss things with manager Howard Kendall. The fee stood at around £1.5 million, but then Spurs put it up to £1.7 million. Souness came on again and asked if we could open up the deal but Paul was happy with the Spurs' personal terms and it looked all over.' But then there was a final call that has never been revealed until now. 'The phone rang in my office and a new club wanted to get in on the transfer deal. It was Manchester United manager Alex Ferguson. But by that time Paul was all set to leave and sign for Spurs. It was decided not to tell him of United's interest and he duly signed for Tottenham Hotspur.'

With a massive injection of £1.7 million into the Maine Road coffers from the Paul Stewart transfer deal the way was now open for Machin to bring in new men for a big push for promotion in that

1988-89 season. 'I felt the team was playing with the right style,' says Machin. 'The resolve was there and now I wanted to bring in some new faces to give us more power and balance.' Before the season started, that gutsy striker Wayne Biggins had arrived from Norwich for £160,000. A new goalkeeper arrived in the likeable shape of Andy Dibble, a £240,000 signing from Luton Town. The defence received a solid new figure in the real-tough form of Brian Gayle, from Wimbledon. Gayle was to prove a tremendous asset in this coming season, not only for his blood and guts performance on the field of play but also for his cavalier presence around the Maine Road scene. During the season further new figures arrived. Goalkeeper Paul Cooper came from Leicester, Gary Megson was a £250,000 signing from Sheffield Wednesday and Carl Bradshaw also arrived from Hillsborough. There was another signing in striker David Oldfield from Luton Town costing £600,000. Nigel Gleghorn, with his superb left-foot touches, came in from Ipswich for £45,000 and if ever there was a snip of a transfer then that was it. Gleghorn had a great season. Aussie striker David Oldfield was the biggest buy of the lot when City splashed out £600,000 to Luton for him in March 1989.

In the penultimate match of that successful season, against Bournemouth at Maine Road, victory would have meant certain promotion. City cruised into a 3-0 half-time lead and their supporters were already celebrating. But a second half collapse let Bournemouth back into the match. As the game moved into injury time with the score now 3-2, Bournemouth were given a shock penalty award. City supporters couldn't bear to watch. But Luther Blissett made no mistake and everything now rested on the last game of the season at Bradford City—a real nerve jangler for the City supporters if ever there was one.

City had to get at least a draw to secure promotion. The fans were full of confidence as they piled out of their coaches outside the Bradford City ground. But with only five minutes of the match remaining, City trailed by a goal to nil and the supporters' nerves were at breaking point. Then, with four minutes to go, Trevor Morley pounced for the equaliser. For Machin, the players and the fans a moment of sheer agony was instantly transformed into ecstasy. It was one big celebration all the way home across the Pennines.

Machin was rightly proud of what he had achieved at Maine Road. He was well served by player-coach John Deehan whom he had brought in from Ipswich. Deehan was shrewd and his quick sense of humour made him a popular figure with the rest of the players. Machin saw his role quite clearly. 'I am the sort of manager who likes to make the established players even better ones and to bring in the youngsters steadily and mould them all into an attractive attacking side.'

Machin felt that now they were in the First Division he could look forward to building up a really good team in the same style as he had done at Norwich. Furthermore, he was delighted to hear chairman Swales express his satisfaction at the way things were going during the close season. 'He made a speech to supporters at a hotel in Warrington,' remembers Machin. 'He said, "It has been a long time since I felt we had some real stability at the club."' It was now that Machin proved he was as honourable to Manchester City as he had been to Norwich when City had first approached him. For both West Ham United and Newcastle United were keen for him to discuss the possibility of joining them. He turned them both down. In fact, another club actually made contact with him at the hotel in Italy where Machin was on holiday. 'Someone pushed a note under my bedroom door,' reveals Machin. 'Two men were waiting to talk to me at the bar. I told them I was only interested in staying with Manchester City.'

To be fair to the chairman, Swales and the City board gave Machin some big money to spend as he prepared for the return to the First Division. Full of confidence, Machin brought in Ian Bishop, an exciting midfielder, from Bournemouth in a swap deal. Next to arrive was striker Clive Allen, for £1.1 million. Allen, the renowned goal-getter was then with the French club Bordeaux.

So the first season back in the top-flight opened in the August of 1989. City made a jittery start, losing three and drawing one of their first four games. But it was a completely different story over the next four games of which they won three, including a stunning victory in the derby against old enemies United at Maine Road on 23 September. United manager Alex Ferguson saw his highly expensive stars go crashing down to a 5-1 defeat. David Oldfield gave City the lead. Trevor Morley and Ian Bishop made it 3-0 by the break. Mark Hughes pulled one back but Oldfield and Andy Hinchcliffe made it five. Massacre! Machin's tactics had worked a treat and the way ahead looked strewn with roses. But another bad patch threw a different complexion on things when City crashed 6-0 at Derby County and were beaten 3-0 at Maine Road the following Saturday by Brian Clough's Nottingham Forest.

Chairman Swales called Machin into his office. 'He told me he was sorry but said, "It just hasn't worked out." I was to go,' says Machin. 'He never actually gave me an exact reason for my dismissal. But I got the feeling he was hinting that I wasn't flamboyant enough for the job. I must say that I never had any arguments with Swales. But considering I had done the job of getting City back into the First Division, I certainly felt angry and badly let down.

'That 5-1 defeat of United had been our absolute highlight. Okay, we still had problems with the side. It was playing in fits and starts and obviously that was irritating. But I was confident we could smooth out the difficulties. I felt that I could have made them as good a side as Norwich given the opportunity—and got them into Europe. That was my plan, but I wasn't given the time.

'Also, I think I had negotiated well with the players we brought in—the wage bill was unbelievably low for a First Division outfit.'

After announcing that Machin was out, Swales said he felt that Machin had failed to communicate with the supporters. So it was back to the managerial drawing board yet again for City, as a bitterly hurt Machin tried to come to terms with the blow of dismissal. Once again it was clearly the spectre of relegation that stampeded the City directors into deciding Machin should go. The two recent confidence-sapping defeats by Derby County, and Nottingham Forest had seen City slump into the relegation zone. But the great thing in City's favour was that there was a top-class candidate available. He was a still young manager with one of the finest records in the game. Yet the best thing of all, as far as City was concerned, was that he was completely unattached. So there would be no haggling to be done regarding his contract with another club.

City turned to the extremely successful Howard Kendall, the man who had built Everton into one of the finest teams in England—and Europe for that matter. Kendall was a free agent after quitting crack Spanish club Athletico Bilbao after a two-year spell. Throughout a distinguished career with Preston North End he had quickly shot himself into the record books when he played in the FA Cup final at Wembley for Preston against West Ham at the tender age of 17—which constituted a record at that time. He moved to Goodison in 1967 to play a versatile and classic role in the great Everton team of that period. Along with two other midfield masters, Colin Harvey and Alan Ball, he was in the side that topped a great 1969-70 season by winning the championship. He left Goodison and played for Birmingham City and then Stoke City before making his first serious move into management when he took over as player-manager at Blackburn Rovers. He showed immediately that he had the qualities of leadership that are required of a top manager and inspired Blackburn to win promotion to the Second Division in the 1979-80 season. In the summer of 1981 he took command at Goodison Park after Everton had fired previous manager Gordon Lee. After surviving an extremely rocky start, Kendall's class shone through and Everton clinched the League Championship in 1985 and 1987, winning the FA Cup in 1984 and being beaten finalists in the League Cup that same season. They won the European Cup Winners Cup in 1985. But he left Everton fans dumbfounded in 1987, insisting that he wanted a fresh challenge and leaving to take over at Athletico Bilbao in Spain.

When Kendall returned to this country two years later and heard his phone ring to find City on the line, he was obviously very interested. 'Manchester City are a very big club,' he says. 'I was keen to stay in the game in the North-west area if possible. Obviously there was no opportunity on Merseyside, and Manchester United had Alex Ferguson. So this was a wonderful chance. It suited me down to the ground to have such an opportunity, having just returned to this country from Spain a few days earlier.'

It was made plain to Howard that the one and only priority was to keep City in the First Division. Chairman Peter Swales was, quite rightly, absolutely delighted to have landed such a big fish as Kendall. 'We have a man whose record speaks for itself,' he said with understandable delight. 'He has done it at the very top and we are looking forward to going places under his expert managership.'

Once again, the new manager realised that there was no open cheque book at the ready, although there was some money available for players. 'I straightaway knew I had to get down to some wheeling and dealing for new and dependable players as quickly as possible,' Kendall told me. 'I had been away for over two years in Spain, but I had talked to John Toshack who was also managing out there and we agreed how important it was to keep in touch with what was happening back home on the football scene. I had done this because I always knew that I would be coming back here. So I had kept in touch with soccer friends over here—especially about what was happening around the North West and what the situation was with players involved there.'

Certainly Kendall immediately impressed the backroom staff at Maine Road from the minute he walked through the door. Ken Barnes, a senior figure at City with his admirable record as a great former skipper and wing-half with City, and now chief scout, was happy at Kendall's arrival. 'His man-management style was superb,' recalls Barnes. 'He had polish and confidence. The younger players, especially, were a little in awe of him which is always a great thing when you are trying to inspire confidence. The senior players had an immediate respect for him. He got everybody up on their toes and the determination was there. The message was that we would keep the club in the First Division. That came over very strongly.'

Kendall went through a veritable whirlwind of transfer work. 'It was quite incredible,' says Barnes. 'At times, I could hardly keep up with who was coming and who was going. But in the end, he got it right and you must give him credit for that.

'I must say that at the time, I did question his judgment of some of the players whom he let leave the club. But he was the manager and he was operating at extraordinary speed.'

Kendall was extremely unfortunate during his playing career never to be capped by England. Likewise, Ken Barnes was constantly described by the press in his playing days as 'the best uncapped wing-half in England'. When Kendall arrived at Maine Road, he joked with Ken, 'Well, you and I certainly have something in common—we never played for our country. But I reckon we know a thing or two about this game, don't we?'

Says Barnes, 'It was his sense of fun and the way he got on with things so directly that made me think the club had a really great chance of going places at long, long last.'

But the fans needed a lot of persuading that Kendall was their new great hope because of the way he brought a steady flood of former Everton players into his squad. The first two arrivals within weeks of Kendall taking command were veteran midfield master-mind Peter Reid, from Queens Park Rangers, and Alan Harper, from Sheffield United. England international Reid had been a master tactician in Kendall's great Everton team and the excellent utility player Harper was also a former Goodison man during Kendall's reign. More former Everton men followed.

If the City fans were a little miffed to see the influx of Kendall's former troops joining the City ranks, then his decision to let Maine Road favourite Ian Bishop go to West Ham United in a swap deal with striker Trevor Morley for winger Mark Ward, really nettled them. Kendall knew full well a lot of these transfer movements would not be popular with the supporters. But he was equally convinced these moves were the only way to save City's First Division life. 'I knew exactly what the capabilities of these players were,' Kendall told me. 'They had done a great job for me before and I knew they were still capable of fulfilling a specific role for me again. I was not prepared to bring in new men I wasn't one hundred per cent sure of. We hadn't time for players who couldn't perform a special task and do it quickly. Peter Reid was absolutely terrific. He was not only a great player to have out there on the field but he was also an extremely steadying influence in the dressing-room. The fans certainly let me know how they felt about Bishop. They loved his style. He was a neat footballer with plenty of skill. But he wasn't the type that I needed in the team at that point because of the position we were in. I had brought Harper in to play as sweeper and he did the job extremely effectively. When I let Bishop go, the chants went up at the next match, "There's only one Ian Bishop". I could understand their disappointment in losing a player who was a special favourite. But I had to do the job I had been brought in to do—keep City in the First Division.'

Another former Everton man came in January 1990 when Kendall signed striker Wayne Clark, from Leicester City. A month later, yet another of Kendall's old boys arrived in the shape of little goal-getter and grafter Adrian Heath, from Aston Villa. Kendall laughs when he recalls how he decided in one game to send on Heath from the substitute's bench to replace another City favourite Steve Redmond. 'The supporters really had a go at that,' remembers Kendall. 'They started chanting, "What the hell's going on?" But we were pulling things round steadily.'

Yet Kendall's next and biggest signing was a tremendous hit with everyone at Maine Road. He pounced in March for the lanky Republic of Ireland striker Niall Quinn, for whom he paid Arsenal £800,000. 'I was absolutely delighted to have got Niall,' says Kendall. 'He was a great player, another excellent influence in the dressing-room. I had the nucleus of a good side already with Niall, Reid and Heath being the type of men the younger players could look up to.'

As City's League position in the First Division table eased, so

Kendall now adopted an attacking stance with a 4-4-2 formation. When Quinn scored in his début in the 1-1 draw with Chelsea at Maine Road in March, the City fans realised everything was going to be alright. 'We clinched our First Division safety with a 1-0 win at Norwich in April with three games of the season left,' recalls Kendall. He must have been especially pleased that the flying Adrian Heath had scored the winner that kept City up.

Kendall had done a great job and chairman Peter Swales could afford to allow himself a smile of triumph. He had brought in one of the finest managers in football, given him his head, and provided the resources to buy a real star like Quinn. It had saved City's First Division skins. The future looked extremely bright now that Kendall had arrived. They were soon drawing up plans for the coming season. There didn't seem a cloud in the sky. Yet Swales and the City supporters were in for a bitter shock not long into the new season.

Kendall decided to strengthen his squad still further in the close season and the chairman and the City board gave him the thumbs up to agree a £900,000 fee with Watford for their exciting goalkeeper Tony Coton. Coton was cheap at the price. He had shown by some absolutely outstanding displays that he was possibly the best goalkeeper in the country.

The new 1990-91 season started sweetly for City with three wins and a draw in the first five matches. The second was a thrilling 1-0 win over Kendall's old club Everton in front of a 31,000 crowd at Maine Road. Ironically, the winner came from ex-Evertonian Adrian Heath so Kendall could afford a satisfied smile. There was further evidence of how highly Kendall was rated. Chairman Peter Swales, who was on the FA International Council, took him to one side and informed him that the FA wished to interview him about the England job. He was one of the men on the FA's short list for the job. Kendall recalls with a smile, 'When the chairman had made it plain he was passing on that information as an FA Councillor, he then asked me as chairman again, "You wouldn't take it, though, would you?" I just laughed and said I wouldn't because I was happy with my job in club management. But I knew it wouldn't come to anything in any case because I was certain that Graham Taylor was the man really ear-marked for the position.'

That's how it turned out of course. But if chairman Swales had breathed a sigh of relief over that, there was a blow coming up shortly that would leave him thunderstruck.

After the early start of the season, Kendall felt well pleased as he took stock of the situation. 'I now had the nucleus of a very good squad,' he says. 'It was the youngsters who pleased me and one in particular—Paul Lake.' Kendall immediately realised that there was a truly remarkable talent. 'He had so much ability it was absolutely stunning,' says Kendall. 'He had balance, control . . . the lot. He was even great in the air. The biggest difficulty with Paul was knowing exactly where his best position lay. Because he could do the lot— attack, defend, even play a midfield role quite brilliantly. I finally felt he was best in the middle of the defence ready to go forward. I rated him in the class of Liverpool's great defender Alan Hansen. He had all the same capabilities and Alan's beautiful style.'

Yet there was heartbreak ahead for Lake. He went down injured, gripping his knee in the game against Aston Villa. 'At that moment, it didn't appear a bad injury and we were just hoping the knee had simply been slightly wrenched,' says Kendall. But a specialist broke the grim news to Lake and City. The injury was a serious one— damaged cruciate ligaments. At the time of writing, Lake is in the middle of a long, arduous comeback campaign which everyone hopes will see him back to his very best. Certainly Kendall knew it was a real blow to lose Lake's services during this, his second, season with City. 'Paul was going to be a vital part of the team, and to lose a player of his ability really was a blow,' says Kendall.

However, City progressed happily through the early part of the season. In October they fought out a thrilling 3-3 draw with United, at Maine Road. Although there was the disappointment of being knocked out of the Rumbelow's League Cup by Arsenal, who won a close game 2-1 at Maine Road, Kendall still seemed well on course for building City into a forceful outfit in the First Division.

But in November chairman Swales received that numbing shock. Kendall told him, 'I'm sorry, I would like to be released from my contract.' There was a clause in Kendall's contract that had been agreed upon by both parties, allowing Kendall to take another opportunity if it should present itself. In Kendall's case, it is probable that Swales and the board felt they had nothing to worry about once the England job had been resolved with Graham Taylor taking over. They had never considered that another club could coax Kendall away. But there was—and that club was Kendall's former love, Everton.

'The chairman asked me if it was a case of money but I said it wasn't,' reveals Kendall. 'The pull of Goodison was too much. I couldn't resist it. I felt that I had done a good job for City. I told the chairman that I was leaving him with a great squad of players and there was a good future ahead if it could be further worked on. I also pointed out that he had a great possible manager in Peter Reid who had been my deputy.'

Kendall also maintains there was no suggestion he was leaving because of the fans' early antagonism towards him regarding the former Everton men he had brought to the club. 'Those ex-Everton players fought their hearts out for Manchester City,' insists Kendall. 'Once they pulled on those famous sky-blue shirts, they were City players through and through. I just wish the supporters could have had the chance to see the tremendous spirit we had in the dressing-room—especially during the first season when they played such a vital part in helping to keep the club in the First Division.'

Kendall departed to return to Goodison Park for a second spell. It was to prove an unhappy return and Kendall eventually resigned and left Everton for a second time recently. But for Swales, it was a bitter blow. On this occasion everyone must have had a lot of sympathy for the City chief. He had brought in a man who was doing a great job and the future had never looked more exciting. Now he again needed a new manager. He quickly decided to heed Kendall's advice and handed the job to no-nonsense Peter Reid.

CHAPTER SIXTEEN

IT WAS EARLY MORNING when the telephone rang. I heard the bubbling voice of Francis Lee at the other end. 'Morning, Alec, have you finally got out of bed, you lazy old so and so?'

Considering that it was still only ten minutes past eight, I judged that a bit of an unkind jibe. But with Franny, you have to take it. He is already out and about around six o'clock every morning of the week, planning, working, contacting people regarding his many businesses. A big part of his life concerns his string of magnificent racehorses kept at his large Stanneylands Stables in rural Cheshire. He is usually out at first light for a gallop. Ironically, it was racing that was to bring us together that very morning. 'Right, if you can get up here inside an hour, I'll take you to Doncaster races,' said Franny.

'Great,' I replied. 'That suits me down to the ground. I want to talk about what I'm writing. I'll be at your house as quick as I can.'

The discussions we were to have during that day at Doncaster racecourse not only set me up for one of the best exclusive soccer stories I have had in my career as a sports writer with the *Daily Mirror*, they also went a long way to finally convincing the former Bolton Wanderers, Manchester City, Derby County and England striker that he could influence the future of the great Maine Road club.

The sun beat down out of a cloudless sky as I rattled the door of Franny's magnificent mansion. A gleaming racing-green Bentley stood in the large courtyard. Also parked there was a blue Mercedes and two other less eyecatching motors. Franny was just finishing a late breakfast. The thing I like most about being in Francis Lee's company is his impish sense of humour. We climbed into the Mercedes a few minutes later and soon Lee swept the car into Ringway Airport car park. 'Just got a little bit of business to discuss,' he told me. 'Now sit still and don't play around with any of the gadgets,' he said, wagging a roguish finger as if admonishing a naughty juvenile.

I looked at the new car telephone and another portable one by the dashboard. 'I'll just make a few calls to New York,' I laughed.

Franny wasn't gone more than 15 minutes. Yet in that time, I am pretty certain his business talks had set up a catering deal that would bring in another nice little windfall for the amazing millionaire sporting businessman. Lee has a truly remarkable feel for high finance and the way to handle it. But he never, ever brags about his string of extraordinary successes that have made him an extremely wealthy man.

As Lee rolled his car towards the entrance for owners and trainers at the Doncaster racecourse, the gate keeper instantly recognised him, and with a quick salute waved our car through. The attendant at the parking lot had a long chat with Franny, who patiently listened as he recalled with obvious affection the great days in Lee's illustrious playing career. 'Well, that's very nice of you to say so,' Franny replied with a grin. 'I just got lucky quite a bit and I'm just hoping my horse is going to get lucky today.'

We mingled among the crowd. I left Lee to chat to his fellow owners for a couple of hours. When his horse got boxed in on the rails and just failed to make the first three, I expected him to be out of humour when we met at the bar later. Not a bit of it. Lee ordered champagne and chicken salads for us and we talked football. I asked him why he didn't get back into the game. I had heard that a few years ago he had considered making a take-over bid for his first club, Bolton Wanderers, and toyed with the idea of installing his great friend Malcolm Allison as manager.

'Yea, I did have a look at that possibility,' he smiled. 'But I can't possibly get involved in football because of my other business commitments—and especially as I am now involved in the horse-racing world. In any case, I'm quite happy not being involved.'

We sipped more champagne and I persisted, 'You have been asked by a lot of people over the last few years to get involved with

Manchester City. Surely, you must have considered it very seriously?
Weren't you tempted?'

Lee grinned. 'You're a rum bugger, Johnson,' he quipped. 'I
hope you're not going to run banner headlines in the *Mirror* tomorrow saying "Lee To Take Over Manchester City".'

I looked at him seriously. 'No, I'm not. But one day soon I hope I
will do. Because it is the headline that thousands and thousands of
City fans have been praying they will read. You are their idol . . .
their one big hope is for you to turn the club around.'

Lee laughed. 'Don't bother trying to persuade me. I've too much
on my plate. But I'll tell you this. I'm sickened to think how low
that great club has sunk. When I think of what we all achieved
under Joe Mercer and Malcolm Allison and to see City struggling . . .
it's enough to make you weep.'

We drove home as Lee had an urgent business appointment that
evening. As he dropped me off near my home after a long, enjoy-
able chat about the good old days when soccer was fun, I said to
Franny, 'I still think the greatest opportunity of your life would be
to lift Manchester City back to greatness. If you do decide it's worth
a crack, I'd like to be the first to run the story—is that okay with
you?'

Lee's infectious laugh came back from inside the car. 'It won't
happen, but if I ever change my mind, you can have the story on
your own for old times' sake.' Then with a cheery wave from
Franny, the blue Mercedes swept out of sight and what had been a
super day in Lee's effervescent company was over.

I went home cheered by the thought that Franny was still toying
with the idea of having a go for control of Manchester City. At no
point had he ever said, 'Out of the question . . . I'll never consider
it.' Also, I had noted, as all experienced journalists do, that there
was a slight reticence in his voice as he delivered his replies to my
questions. I felt convinced in my mind that this mercurial footballer
who had burst upon the soccer scene as a battling 16-year-old was
tormented by City's miserable showing while big neighbours
United were storming back to the top of the tree again. I had heard
Franny admit time and again how much it hurt him to see the club
struggling year after year and to see how United, now under the
inspirational guidance of chairman Martin Edwards and the new
manager Alex Ferguson, who was, with the vast financial resources
Edwards gave him, giving United that champions' look.

Our trip to Doncaster took place in August before the start of the 1993-94 season. Within a matter of weeks City were playing badly and Swales decided to act. He clearly realised, a fellow director told me, that he had made a mistake in appointing Reid and the aggressive Sam Ellis as his aide, and he also knew that public pressure was now building against him. The City fans were depressed at the catalogue of sackings of managers by Swales—the very man who was responsible for hiring them. They were not producing the successful team the fans were screaming for ever since the great Mercer days.

So now Swales decided on a new appointment. He would bring in John Maddock, a former sports editor of a big Sunday newspaper and a lifelong friend. He and Maddock had kept in close touch since their first meeting when Swales was chairman of non-League club Altrincham more than 20 years ago and Maddock wrote stories on non-League football for a national daily newspaper. Nevertheless this seemingly quite baffling appointment left the ordinary City supporter puzzled.

A current director of long standing told me, 'When he told me of his decision, I could not believe it, but then after further consideration I came to the firm belief that his judgment in controlling Manchester City had slipped badly.' Nonetheless Maddock came breezing into Maine Road and held several press conferences, giving the clear implication that he was a man with power. Yet from the outset it became patently clear that the tactics of Swales and Maddock were destined to failure. Neither was to realise how completely they had misjudged not only the feeling of the fans but also the players. Maddock told the waiting press, 'I have the right to hire and fire.' That almost shock observation was followed by a terse statement that Peter Reid and Sam Ellis had been dismissed. City fans reeled from yet another managerial assassination. Yet they were to be even more stunned by the news on radio and television that Maddock had headed southwards to a secret destination to bring back the new man who was to be the salvation of Maine Road. Speculation swept from one name to another, with Gerry Francis of Queens Park Rangers being the popular front-runner. After hours of this extraordinary guessing game the new manager of Manchester City was announced and most fans said, 'Who?' It was the likeable Brian Horton, manager of Oxford United. Now Horton was in—but he was going to have to work under extreme difficulties. The exit of Reid and Ellis and the shock arrival of Horton all in a matter of days left the City fans baffled.

Maddock had been a successful Northern sports editor of *The People*. No one was disputing that. But the outcry against the appointment was because he had never had any experience in handling a top League football club like Manchester City. Sports writer Norman Wynne, who worked with Maddock at *The People*, says 'John was a great newspaperman but I have no doubt whatsoever that he must have found it difficult coming into the City scene as an administrator. I think it was a big mistake for Swales to bring anyone into a position of power in the club when that person had never been involved in the running of a big football set-up like City's. I think that swung the whole thing against Swales, and helped Lee's consortium just when they needed it.' Ken Barnes, the former skipper, coach and chief scout at the club agreed. 'It really was a bad appointment because people naturally resented anyone coming into Maine Road like that when they had had no previous experience in running a football club.'

Once again it was early morning when my phone rang and I heard Franny at the other end as chirpy as ever. 'Like to come over for a chat?' he asked.

It was another bright day. The date was Tuesday, 31 August 1993. I was delighted. I was gathering facts and figures for this book about City from Mercer's glory days up to the present time. I realised Franny, who had already been extremely helpful with reminiscences during our trip to the races, had some further information which might be of some help. Soon I was sitting in his superb lounge and I slipped my notebook out to take some valuable notes.

'Put that away,' Franny grinned. 'This isn't about your book. It is just to put you in the picture as I promised I would.' I felt a genuine surge of elation. He fixed me with that waspish grin and added, 'I'm going for it. I want to take over at Maine Road. It is something I just cannot resist. It is not about money or power. So many people have appealed to me to make it the sort of football club they used to love. I think, with all the support from a host of loyal City backers, that we can make it. I'm certainly going to give it my best shot.'

His phone rang and I was left with my own thoughts on what this could mean to the future of Manchester City. I was convinced that it would be a new era. It would be the way forward after years of frustration. Now I had a red-hot exclusive burning in my pocket. But Lee wagged his warning finger. 'Hold it until our consortium are ready to go. We must not let this go public until exactly the right moment.'

I spent the next five days in mental agony. Franny was moving discreetly from one business associate to another and setting up further plans. I felt utterly convinced, despite all his promises, that someone would spring a leak. 'Stop panicking,' he told me with that infectious chuckle. 'Everything is going according to plan.' After further nightmares of waking up in a sweat believing the rest of the national press had overheard a conversation and dropped lucky on the story, I got the final call from Franny. 'Okay, you can run the story tomorrow morning,' he told me happily.

It was the word that Keith Fisher, the go-ahead sports editor of the *Daily Mirror* had been waiting for. He gave Lee's dramatic bid for Manchester City the full *Mirror* treatment with glaring head-lines, brilliant pictures and superb artwork from his talented sports staff team. When the *Mirror* told the waking Manchester sports public and especially the City supporters that Francis Lee was to take on chairman Peter Swales and the rest of the board in a bid for power at Maine Road there was a mixed reaction. The genuine City fans were delirious. They still hailed Lee as one of City's greats, knew of his marvellous business empire that had been built up by sheer hard work, and knew best of all that Franny was a fighter. But the doubters and the sceptics shrugged their shoulders insisting, 'It will never work because Swales will never allow it.'

Swales held 30 per cent of the club's shares along with his friend and businessman Stephen Boler, who owned another 30 per cent. Another 20 per cent had been taken up by the brewery, Greenalls, who have a sponsorship deal with the club. Swales and Boler had an agreement that neither would sell without close consultation with the other. It looked like an unbreakable alliance.

I was fascinated to see Lee's big ally a few days later—another former City player and another extremely astute and successful entrepreneur, Colin Barlow. It was the ice-cool, polished Barlow who, in a very short time, was to convince me that he and Franny had formed what was going to be a winning team. If I had had any misgivings over the venture, they all disappeared as I stood sipping a drink in Barlow's sumptuous mansion, Compstall Hall, and listen-ing to him and Franny setting out their strategy. As I patted the huge head of Colin's Great Dane which nuzzled close for attention, and listened to the pair talking, I thought how ironic it was that these two former City players should now be bidding to take over their old club.

When the news broke on 6 September that Francis Lee was throwing his hat into the ring and taking on Manchester City chairman Peter Swales and his directors, the ordinary Maine Road supporters reacted with extraordinary speed. They immediately hurled their massive support behind their former goal-grabbing hero. It was, as one of them, Derek Partridge said, 'A heaven-sent chance we have waited so long for . . . a chance we simply mustn't miss because we won't get it again.' Businessman Partridge contacted Tony Meehan, another solid City fan. These two now joined forces with another rabid City follower, Alan Tapper, the landlord at the Star Inn at Failsworth. They immediately came up with the title for their drive behind the Francis Lee bid for Maine Road power—the 'Forward With Franny' campaign.

Thousands and thousands rallied to the cause. Long years of sheer frustration had meant that there was hardly a Manchester City supporter who did not want a change in the boardroom. The very thought of former City hero Francis Lee moving into the chair captured their imaginations in a flash. 'It was amazing,' says Alan Tapper. 'All our telephone numbers were passed around the City supporters and in no time at all there was a never-ending stream of calls promising 100 per cent support for the Francis Lee campaign. I knew we would have a pretty good backing. But the enormous volume of fans coming behind us was truly inspiring and very, very moving.

'It was as if they had been waiting for over 15 years for someone like Lee to come and lead the club out of the dark days. We knew it was going to be a long, long battle. But we were determined we would win. Franny's initial remark stuck in our minds all through the campaign—especially when things seemed to be going against us. He had said, "No matter what happens, we will not go away. We are going to win, no matter how long it takes." That gave us so much heart and every one of the thousands of fans kept right behind Franny.'

From the first day to the last, this vast band of followers remorselessly campaigned for Lee to be chairman of the club. In vain, the City board appealed against the relentless pressure that bore down on them. There were claims of dirty tricks and aggressive, bullying tactics as the 'Forward with Franny' campaign mounted one demonstration after another. 'Yet,' says Partridge with justified pride, 'there was not one single arrest by the police during all our demonstrations.' Partridge recalls his early days at Maine Road when his father, who sadly died last year, first took him to watch City when he was only eight years old. 'About ten years ago, my father said to me, "I wish we could find someone who could wake the sleeping giant and make City great again." When we heard through the sports pages of the *Daily Mirror* that Francis Lee was prepared to have a go at taking control it was like a dream come true . . . an opportunity too good to miss. When Tony Meehan came to my home to hold our first interview with the media, who wanted to know our plans, little did we know just what lay ahead. We would hardly have been able to guess that in 14 weeks time Peter Swales would have departed Maine Road and Francis Lee would be installed as the new chairman.'

Yet the immediate reaction from the City board to Lee's bid for power was that they were in no way willing to sit down and open negotiations. Despite repeated appeals from Lee's ace ally, former City player Colin Barlow, to at least listen to their overtures, the City board were adamant there would be no talks. But if people within Manchester City believed that that was the end of the matter they could not have been more wrong. Being an outsider when it came to big business matters, I admit I was a little nonplussed by events. But when I called in for a chat and a quiet drink with Franny, he immediately dispelled any doubts I had. Our talks were constantly interrupted by a stream of calls from business friends, advisors and close pals rallying to the cause. The reaction had surprised even Franny. Everyone wanted to rush to the cause. 'Well, we have got the show on the road,' Franny told me with that famous grin. 'Now we have got to grind the opposition into the ground.' That was the style and determination of Franny. He set about dislodging chairman Peter Swales and his business ally Stephen Boler, the two main shareholders. Right across the country, people in football were saying the same thing—'It can't be done. No one can shift Swales from the City chairman's seat.' No one, that is, except Francis Lee. The man believes that you can't lose if you try hard enough. Certainly, he and Barlow got their message across to the fans in the next few days. 'We have started something and we are going to finish it no matter how long it takes,' roared Lee defiantly. The fans loved it. The 'Forward with Franny' followers were soon rallying to the cause in a big way that was clearly worrying the City hierarchy.

The campaign quickly swelled in size and impact. There were radio and television appearances by members of the campaign and many former City players like Mike Summerbee lent their voices to the storm of protests over the City board's refusal to get down to discussions with the Lee consortium. Lee's first appearance at the ground since announcing his determination to take over City was before the home game against Queens Park Rangers. He received a delirious welcome from an enormous gathering as he struggled to reach the front entrance through the back-slapping well-wishers. 'In all that time, I did not hear one fan saying he was against Lee,' says Derek Partridge. 'He was the only man the supporters wanted and it was extraordinary to all of us how the City board just refused to face up to the truth—the fans had had enough of them.'

City's home game against Queens Park Rangers was a major milestone in the campaign. This was the first demonstration of so many that the 'Forward with Franny' campaigners were to hold. Those in the Swales camp shrugged their shoulders and insisted, 'It is only a token gesture. They will go away in a couple of weeks.' But they completely misread the mood of these steadfast City supporters. They were hell-bent on victory and said so again and again on radio and television. They were determined they were going to win no matter how long it took. Says Partridge, 'Initially, we had been warned by experts that if Franny made a full bid and it was turned down, then he would have to wait a full year before he could make another one. It was a sickening thought. But Lee had promised the fans, "We will not go away, no matter how long it takes." That spurred us on. We were resolved utterly to keep up non-stop support for Franny for as long as was necessary. If it meant years than that's the way it would be.'

There were more and more demonstrations. There was a protest at the board's refusal to budge involving the City supporters holding up lighted candles before and after the home game with Oldham Athletic. The club protested that this would be a fire risk. But solicitors contacted by the campaign organisers were informed by the police that as the Kippax Stand, where the demonstration was planned, was made of steel, they could go ahead. Local radio

147

stations were constantly bombarded with calls from City supporters promising their support for Lee and calling for talks to begin. There was even the extraordinary sight of the Reverend Jim Burns, Vicar of St Peter's Church in Chorley and life-long City supporter, pictured in the paper, praying for Peter Swales to quit as chairman. It now seemed to the beleaguered City board that maybe even divine help was coming to Lee's side.

But what must have really worried the City directors was when the 'Forward with Franny' campaign planners made their next move in this never-ending offensive. For this was going to hit the board where they would feel it most—at the bank. Derek Partridge recalls, 'We asked all fans to refrain from buying early season tickets which we knew would be a severe financial blow for the club. I firmly believe that this was the big turning point in our struggle to impress upon the City board that we really could hurt them badly. We were now proving they would be in real trouble if they didn't see sense and co-operate with the Lee consortium.'

By early January it became clear that the City board could stand the pressure no longer. The team, badly hampered by injuries, was having a bitterly disappointing run and rapidly slumped into the relegation zone. They had already been knocked out of the Coca-Cola Cup by Nottingham Forest and it was clear that the likeable and hard-working manager Brian Horton was now under almost intolerable pressure coming from both on and off the field. At last the word came that there would be talks between the two sides. The 'Forward with Franny' members were jubilant. Victory seemed close at hand. The first meeting broke up with promising statements from both parties. Then on Thursday, 13 January, it was announced there was to be a further meeting that day. It was to be held at a Cheshire hotel and it was unanimously expected that agreement would be reached for Lee to take over. In fact Lee, who had been holidaying in Barbados, flew back specially to be on hand for what everybody now expected would be the end of the story.

The *Manchester Evening News* actually ran a story that Lee had triumphed and was the new chairman of Manchester City. But by mid-afternoon the meeting suddenly broke up with the terse statement saying no agreement had been reached. Recalls Alan Tapper, 'We all believed it was a foregone conclusion. But when the news filtered through during the afternoon that it was all off, fans bombarded the "Forward with Franny" telephone numbers wanting to know what was going on. Everybody had been on cloud nine and yet now we had all hit rock bottom. The feeling was that the City board had pulled a fast one or worse, as a rumour was put about that the Lee consortium hadn't enough cash after all.'

City's exultant mass of supporters had already been planning elaborate celebrations for the next home game against Arsenal on the Saturday. Now this news left them devastated—especially when that rumour got around. In fact, it was utterly untrue. It was Lee's financial advisors who had advised the Lee consortium to withdraw temporarily as they were unhappy with some aspects of City's finances, including large loans from the bank.

But gloom still hung over Maine Road during the match against Arsenal, which was drawn 1-1. As the fans streamed homewards there was an air of despondency. Lee had returned immediately to resume his break with his family in Barbados and Colin Barlow had had to fly to Milan to solve a personal business problem that had cropped up.

Word reached the 'Forward with Franny' campaign organisers within the next 24 hours that everything was on hold but Lee was still confident of victory. But many of the supporters were still bitterly despondent. They questioned whether, after being so incredibly close to victory, Lee could make the final breakthrough into the City boardroom and claim the chairman's chair.

Well, if they were unsure, Lee certainly wasn't. By telephone he was carefully setting up the final deal that was to bring him winging home from Barbados to sweep into power. Although the fans thought his chances had gone, the amazing man from Westhoughton, Bolton, was about to win the battle for Manchester City. The streets were about to ring with cheers for an incredible victory—a victory won against all the odds.

The news that thousands of patient Manchester City fans had been waiting to hear finally broke on the morning of Thursday, 3 February 1994. The City board announced that they would be meeting with Lee's consortium the next day to settle the final details of the takeover of the club. At Friday lunchtime Lee flew into Ringway Airport after breaking his holiday in Barbados for the second time in a bid to end the deadlock. Yet, once again, there was to be no quick announcement that the deal had been completed. In fact, it was to take ten agonising hours of negotiations, first at offices in the city centre and then at a Cheshire hotel, before a jubilant Lee

149

and Colin Barlow emerged at 12.24 a.m. to announce that Francis Lee, after a five-month battle, had won his fight for control of Manchester City.

Lee told me later, 'That moment was worth waiting for. It was worth all the hassle, all the upsets, all the bitter disappointments along the way, because it meant that not just we, the consortium, had won. It meant that the Manchester City fan had won. It was a quite tremendous performance by thousands and thousands of supporters who had been willing us to win. They had proved by their determined stand behind us that they could influence who they wanted in control of their football club. I don't think that has ever happened before in football.' Lee was quick to promise those supporters, 'One of our first priorities will be to appoint a director who will be responsible for the well-being and care of the supporters who have given me such a great backing.'

For Barlow, it was a particular moment of triumph, just as it was for astute businessman and multi-millionaire John Dunkerley, who now lives in Spain. Dunkerley proved an admirable ally for Lee and Barlow, not only giving them vital powerful financial support in the takeover struggle, but helping to boost morale along the way. It was a wonder Lee was still on his feet. He had been 30 hours without sleep since leaving Barbados to complete his dream ticket—the chairmanship of the club he once played for with such panache.

So the scene was set the next day for a carnival atmosphere at Maine Road, where City were to meet Ipswich in a Premiership game. Nearly 30,000 fans were in the ground hours before the kick-off. A host of former great City players waved to the fans. A plane towing the banner 'Welcome Francis Lee' flew overhead and a stream of thousands of balloons floated skywards at ten minutes to three. It was the moment City supporters had been waiting for. Francis Lee, with a huge grin on his face, tanned by the Barbados sunshine, stepped into the directors' box and raised both hands above his head in salute as the huge roar rang out to welcome the new supremo of the club—the chairman chosen by the people. Despite the horror of going behind 1-0, the City players made it a true gala occasion when David Rocastle, with some glorious footwork, provided Gary Flitcroft with a juicy pass for the winning goal which the exultant crowd had been screaming for.

For chairman Lee and managing director Barlow, the battle for Manchester City is over. Now they have to build for the future.

150

'There is so much to be done,' Lee told me. 'But together, the players, the directors and the supporters can make this a truly great club again if we all pull together.'

I believe Lee will take Manchester City on to a golden era such as the club has not seen since the days of Mercer and Allison.

CHAPTER SEVENTEEN

FRANCIS LEE, former Manchester City and England star and self-made multi-millionaire, is surely the greatest rags-to-riches story that British football has ever seen. The kid from a humble upbringing in the backstreets of Westhoughton near Bolton, has—thanks to a prodigious talent and undying determination to win through against all the odds—gained control of his old club Manchester City.

Lee's life story reads like that famous comic hero *Roy Of The Rovers*. But his extraordinary exploits in the world of soccer are real—not fiction. Lee has played in mesmerising manner to thrill old and young alike. His swashbuckling style has captured the admiration of millions over the thrill-packed years of his playing career. Equally, the thousands of Manchester City fans have been biting their finger-nails as Lee's battle to gain control of the struggling Maine Road club raged for five long months. Now, along with his big ally and friend Colin Barlow, another goalscoring right winger with City in the '50s, Lee is about to embark on his biggest adventure of all. He aims to build the great old Maine Road set-up into one of the most successful clubs in the land, to bring back the dash and flair that he and his great team-mates showed in the wonderful era of manager Joe Mercer and coach Malcolm Allison.

Along with the startled thousands who witnessed it, I shall never forget Lee's remarkable début for Bolton at the tender age of 16. It was fitting that the date was 5 November 1960, for if ever an unknown kid was to produce a display of glorious fireworks, this was it.

How ironic that the City team had brought a massive following to Burnden Park that afternoon. It was a red-hot atmosphere, a bubbling cauldron of soccer excitement that would surely have daunted any other 16-year-old. But there was no stagefright about the stocky figure of the determined Francis Lee. Not even the presence at his side of none other than the mighty Nat Lofthouse, Bolton's great England striker, known as the Lion of Vienna, seemed to bother him in the least. The ironic and fateful twist to this match was that the man on the right wing for Manchester City in Lee's début match against them was none other than Colin Barlow. Like Lee, he was a powerful player with a marked ability for cracking in thrilling goals. Certainly Barlow has a keen picture of Lee's first game etched firmly in his memory. Lee was bursting with confidence and determination. 'Any other 16-year-old coming out to play in his first game in a match packed with famous players like Nat Lofthouse, Bert Trautmann and Denis Law would have been just happy to try to go through the game without making any mistakes, easing his way through a difficult début,' says Barlow. 'But not Franny. He startled everybody that day—not just the crowd but the players as well—by his sheer cockiness. He traded tackles as hard as any of our big defenders could make. He was whacking at anything that moved. The Bolton fans loved it. But he got a bit carried away by all the excitement and made a clumsy foul and was booked. Yet that was only sheer exuberance on his part. He wasn't a dirty player, anyone could see that.'

Bolton's Stanley gave Wanderers the lead and from a corner by Stevens it was young Lee who sent the Bolton fans wild when he darted in to plant a flashing header past the celebrated Trautmann. The great Denis Law pulled one back for City. But again it was Lee who played the key role in settling the match when his pinpoint corner found the head of Nat Lofthouse who nodded the third goal past a helpless Trautmann.

Lee just shrugs modestly and recalls, 'I was just lucky. I gave it all I had. I have been lucky in that I can never recall being nervous about a game, no matter how big the occasion.' But Barlow insists Lee made a tremendous impact that day. 'It was a stunning début,' says Barlow who recalled another game when he faced the legendary Bolton full-back Tommy Banks. Tommy was at the end of his career, but still a superb, seasoned campaigner—one of a long line of tough, uncompromising defenders Bolton produced in those great days of the Wanderers. Says Barlow with a wry grin, 'I had got past him quite a few times and in the second half I was darting past him again when he sent me crashing over the touchline, down across the dirt track at the side of the pitch and over the pailings and into the crowd. I came scrambling back with bloodied knees and was livid and screamed at him that it was a miracle I hadn't broken my neck, never mind a leg. He just gave me that stony stare. But after the full-time whistle as we were going off, I felt a friendly arm go round my shoulders. It was Tommy. "Colin, good luck in your career," he said to me. "I'm sorry, lad, but I just couldn't let you keep on doing that to me." I forgave him and I have never forgotten the gesture Tommy made. He was a real pro.'

Here is another parallel, for Barlow had also scored on his début on the City right wing, on 28 August, the opening match of the 1957-58 season, against Chelsea at Stamford Bridge. Unlike the nerveless Franny, Colin was full of butterflies before the game. 'There was a crowd of 43,000 and I was quivering with nerves,' he recalls. 'I was wearing a pair of boots given to me by the great Don Revie. Mine had been very worn and Don had noticed and had a spare pair. I was still in the reserves at that point and for a player of Don's calibre to take the trouble over the future of an unknown youngster was wonderful.' Those boots were to prove lucky for Barlow, who recalls, 'The match was a real thriller and we won 3-2. I scored and I will never forget the ball coming across the face of the goal toward me. It seemed to take an eternity to reach me where I was standing. I had to hit it with my left leg which normally was just the one I used for standing on. But at last it was there and I just swung and hoped. When I saw it flowing down the back of the net and heard the crowd's cheers, I only took a couple of seconds to dash back to the halfway line in my celebration dance.' Those moments are worth more than words can express. Players can relive them on a starlit night and they flame again.

So Lee and Barlow seemed destined to unite to change it all. The later union between Lee and Barlow was brought about by a former City director Sydney Rose. Says Barlow, 'Sydney came to my house and said Franny had been horrified at recent events at Maine Road. Most of the former members of the great Mercer-Allison side had been appalled at the way three great City stalwarts had been summarily dismissed since new manager Peter Reid and his assistant Sam Ellis had been appointed.' Former great skipper and coach

155

Ken Barnes had been relieved of his post as chief scout after having brought a constant stream of talent to the club. Also dismissed from his position as coach was Glyn Pardoe, the former top defender in the great Mercer side. The third was the highly popular physio-therapist Roy Bailey whose playing career had been cruelly cut short by injury when he was still a youngster on the Maine Road playing staff.

The treatment of the long-serving Barnes and loyal Bailey had already enraged the City supporters. But the decision to sever Glyn Pardoe's connection with the club was the cruellest blow of all. Pardoe was pure gold and had an impeccable record during Mercer's magical days. Pardoe, a shrewd and rock-solid defender who also portrayed vital flashes of attacking power that were to prove vital to City at crucial moments, was in the thick of the battle every inch of the way. He played 303 League games and picked up an FA Cup-winning medal, a League Championship medal and League Cup winning medal. Glyn is a cousin of Alan Oakes who played an equally important role in that part of City's exciting and highly successful story. But the dedicated Pardoe's career as a City player was to end in the saddest way.

It came in the derby battle between City and United at Old Trafford on 12 December 1970. It was an afternoon of exhilarating triumph for City's fans. City were in rampant form and tore United to shreds. Franny Lee scored a dazzling hat-trick and the marauding Doyle grabbed the other goal for a heady 4-1 victory in the strong-hold of the old enemy. The game was marred by an incident when United superstar George Best tackled Pardoe, who went down in agony and had to be stretchered off. Temperatures ran sky high in the City camp. In all fairness to Best, he stayed on the field and went to great lengths to express his sorrow at the incident that ultimately finished brave Pardoe's career. Best attempted to enter City's dressing-room after the match to express his sorrow at the outcome of the tackle. But Allison tells me he was so emotionally worked up over the injury to Pardoe that he threw a mug of tea at Best, who discreetly withdrew.

It was a sad night for Pardoe but it could have been an even graver situation, for he was rushed to hospital where a specialist battled to save his injured leg from amputation. 'It was only the wizardry of the orthopaedic surgeon that saved his leg,' Roy Bailey and others recall of that night of drama. Says Glyn today, 'Okay, it was a bit of a late tackle and it cost me dearly. But I suppose that is the way it goes in the hard game of professional soccer. I am just glad that I was involved in so much of what were the richest days of Manchester City since the war or at any time, I suppose.'

Barnes, Bailey and even more so Pardoe had given so much to the club and yet now they were being shown the door. Lee felt it was time something was done to stop the humiliating decline of one of the greatest clubs in football. The appointment of former sports journalist John Maddock as general manager and the subsequent firing of Reid and Ellis was 'the last straw' as far as Franny was concerned, Rose told Barlow.

Amazingly, Barlow and Lee hadn't had any connection with one another, other than exchanging a word of greeting at get-togethers for former City players. But Rose had explained to Lee that Barlow had an impeccable City pedigree. Why not get together and talk over a strategy? Barlow was immediately enthralled. 'I knew of Franny's exceptional qualifications as a brilliant businessman and you didn't have to tell me about his fighting qualities. I'd seen those at first hand on the field of play.'

Barlow said he would be delighted to talk with Franny. The next day Lee rang and with his usual bluntness asked Colin, 'Have you any thoughts on turning things around at Manchester City?' It was soccer history in the making. Barlow said he most certainly had and it was time they had a meeting and talked the whole business through. So the meeting was arranged at a cottage at the side of the 18th green at Romiley Golf Club. 'We chatted away,' says Barlow, 'and it was immediately clear that we both felt exactly the same way about things at Maine Road. We agreed that matters had been disastrous over many, many years. We both felt the City fans deserved a better deal than the raw one they had had to suffer over the last ten or 15 seasons. We talked out a plan of campaign and it went from there. We had got the bit between our teeth and we were determined to see it through to the bitter end. We were utterly confident we would win.'

Lee's extraordinary ability on the football field has only been matched by his genius in the world of big business but it was in his early days as a first-teamer at Bolton Wanderers that the canny Franny made his first sortie into the business world. It didn't seem a big deal at the time. In fact, many of his Bolton team-mates thought he was nuts. Lee set off on his afternoons after training, collecting waste paper. First he did it with a barrow, then with a second-hand van. A cheery figure in a pair of overalls, Lee steadily began to build up a business that he would eventually sell for many millions of pounds. But he didn't just stop there. He opened a launderette in his native Westhoughton. 'I had seen people waiting at bus stops with their washing in plastic bags,' recalls Franny. 'They had to go into Bolton if they wanted to use a launderette. So I opened one up in Westhoughton.'

Like every other venture that Lee went into, business boomed. He next opened a hairdressing salon. By the time he had moved to Manchester City his business was very large. It required a lot of handling and involved several people making vital decisions. Lee had to trust someone with a major part of his rapidly expanding empire. But in the autumn of 1969 he received a call from a sharp-eyed accountant who had been checking through the business's recent records. He told Lee something that set the alarm bells ringing. Lee immediately realised that someone had let him down badly.

'When we had checked through everything the full impact of what had happened hit me. We were almost broke. But not only that, we were heavily in debt. There was an enormous amount of money that had gone missing. It was my worst nightmare come true.' The first thing Franny had to do was mortgage his home. He held emergency talks with his bank manager. The official had every confidence in Lee's extraordinary business ability to extricate himself from the mess in which his company now found itself. Someone had filched funds. So it wasn't as if Lee's business was fail-ing. Lee himself called in everyone to whom his firm now owed money and told them bluntly, 'Give me 12 months and I will pay back to you every penny. As it stands, if you press me now, all I am entitled to pay you back is 20p for every pound owed. I want to see that you get every penny back that I owe you.' Like the bank manager, his business associates knew Lee would be as good as his word, even though pulling things around in only one year seemed far too optimistic to hope for. But with the help of his family and close friends, Lee set about putting it right. He went to City manager Joe Mercer to ask for time to allow him to get his company back on its feet. This was Lee the fighter!

Joe Mercer, ever the father figure, insisted Franny be given all the leave from his duties at the club that he needed. 'Get it sorted out,' was Joe's message. Malcolm Allison immediately lent a compassionate ear and the two men told Lee they would help him in any way they could regarding switching his training schedules if necessary so that Lee could give further time to his business affairs.

Every week Lee was allowed a day away from the club so that he could fly to Scandinavia to set up new deals for his paper business. It was a situation that would have worn down lesser skilled men than Lee. But even he admits, 'I was having difficulty sleeping. Everything seemed to have come apart at the seams. Yet I was determined I was going to pull it around no matter how much effort it took.' Amazingly, despite all the relentless pressure bearing down on him through those long months of agony, Lee continued to be as dazzling as ever on the field of play. 'I think it was only during those 90 minutes of a match that I was able to put my worries behind me and relax,' says Franny. 'Also, I was really fired up mentally. I played with an extra abandon and the goals kept coming. It was my way of thanking Joe and Malcolm for their understanding and help with the problems I had been facing.'

By the end of the 12 months that Lee had promised his creditors he would pay them back, he had been as good as his word. Yet, with typical iron resolution, Lee wouldn't simply sit back, wipe his brow or take a breather. He was determined to build his business back to the high position of profitability it had been in before the money had been syphoned away. This now entailed tremendous travelling, not only his weekly trips to Scandinavia, but by car all over this country. He drove over 50,000 miles a year and, inevitably, something had to give. One night Lee was driving down the motorway to Birmingham. He nodded off at the wheel through sheer exhaustion. The next thing he knew there was a massive bang and, as he sprang awake, he saw three lanes of car headlights glaring at him. He realised with horror that he was on the grass of the centre reservation. 'There were no central crash barriers at that time—and I was facing back the way I had come. My heart was nearly jumping out of my shirt,' says Franny, recalling the shock of it all. 'It was sheer exhaustion, and I realised that I must have been within an inch of being killed and, even worse, killing someone else.' But for fate smiling on Francis Lee that night, he could so easily have perished in an horrific crash and football and Manchester City would have been very much the poorer.

Lee decided he really wanted to steer his business into the big time. He went to see his bank manager at Westhoughton only to find that he had retired. Now he faced a completely fresh face sitting in the manager's chair. 'Yet amazingly, when I asked him for a £200,000 loan, he just smiled and gave me the thumbs-up sign,' says Lee. 'I never forgot him for that. A lot of people knock bank managers. But they have some very difficult decisions to make.'

By the summer of 1976, Lee's businesses had grown dramatically and he was now in the millionaire's league in a big way, though still the same modest Bolton lad. At long last he decided it was time for a complete break. What better time, he thought, to do a little fishing and swimming in the beautiful scenery of Scotland? 'I decided to go for a week or so at the farm of a pal of mine, Mike Stewart. It was a spot called Pitlochry and was a famous location for good fishing. Running the business so hard had really worn me out. I loved it up there.'

One very hot, sunny day in June, Lee sauntered up the riverbank. He was all alone and happy with his thoughts now that he had rebuilt his business and was enjoying his football as much as ever with Derby County, whom he had joined for £100,000 in 1974. 'It was so warm, I put on my shorts and decided to go for a swim in the river,' recalls Lee. He plunged in and, after a little aimless swimming around, decided to swim up to the bridge at the head of the river. But although he was a strong swimmer, Lee realised with surprise that the bridge was not getting any larger as he strove to reach it—in fact it was getting smaller. 'The current, as strong as it was, was carrying me back down towards a whirlpool,' says Lee. 'I made a tremendous effort to beat the force of the current, but I just couldn't do it. It was now that it registered with me that I had got a very serious problem. I was determined to try to keep cool and not lose my nerve, yet the current was carrying me backward, alarmingly. My mind kept saying, "Don't panic . . . don't panic." I decided to try to swim to the point where I had got into the water originally, but once again I couldn't make any headway no matter how hard I tried.' Now Lee was in the grip of the whirl-pool. Desperately, he tried to keep his head above water. 'I was really panicking by now,' remembers Lee. 'I was being sucked down and trying hopelessly to get out. I realised, I know now, that I wasn't going to make it. Suddenly my whole world became amazingly serene and there was a golden glow around me. A voice said in my head, "After all that has happened, you have just gone and blown your life."'

Unknown to Lee, his friend, Bill Openshaw and another acquaintance had come down along the bank carrying a rod for Lee to do some fishing. Openshaw was now racing along the bank, staring in horror at Lee's plight. Just alongside was the boathouse which was always firmly locked over the weekend. They raced to it, praying that maybe, by some miracle, it might be open. It was. Callum, the boat keeper, had FORGOTTEN to lock it that weekend, though he could never recall not having locked or bolted it before. Bill quickly pushed the boat into the middle of the river, grabbed Lee and hauled him aboard.

At first, they feared maybe they were too late but on the riverbank Lee's colour slowly began to return. He spent a period in hospital where he was taken by ambulance. When he had fully recovered, Lee reveals, 'I went to the Ballenlough Inn and drank five pints of lemonade. Evidently, when you have been truly scared, you get a raging thirst.' That was a second frightening brush with death for Lee. His down-to-earth mother just smiled when she heard of his latest ordeal. 'You're like a cat,' she told Franny. 'You've got seven lives left.'

CHAPTER EIGHTEEN

THERE IS no better man to turn to if you want to know about Manchester City's adventures over the past 40 years than the irrepressible former captain Ken Barnes. Ken, a midfield architect of some of the best attacking football seen from a Manchester City team, has been in the thick of the action in one capacity or another almost continually. He played a major role and became an inspirational skipper for years before taking over as player-manager of Wrexham. He inspired the Welsh club to win promotion to the Third Division in his first season there.

But he returned to Maine Road as a coach. At one point, when Malcolm Allison was dismissed in his second spell at City in 1980, Ken took over briefly as caretaker manager. In November 1974 he was appointed chief scout as successor to the much loved and highly talented Harry Godwin. Barnes proved invaluable to City in discovering and grooming some of the finest crops of youngsters in football. Many of them came through into the first team, making a big impact and then bringing the club a large and much needed influx of cash when City transferred them to other clubs. Barnes was literally worth his weight in gold to City for the way he found the kids who were sold at a vast profit.

Barnes has City in his blood. 'From the first day I walked in, I just loved the place,' he grins. 'It was just wonderful to go down there day after day. I felt so lucky to be playing football for a living. There wasn't a fortune to be made in the game in those days as there is now for those who play in the Premier League. There were no massive contracts. There were no agents, nor were there television cameras peering at you from every angle both during and after a match. When I started we were on £20 a week plus winning bonuses. But the big difference as against today's professional football was the size of the crowds. The derby clashes at Maine Road were full houses of over 63,000 in the '50s and those sort of massive attendances made for indescribable atmosphere. There was so much noise you couldn't hear yourself think.

'Yet it was a precarious way of life in a way. You never knew if injury might cut your career short. You wondered, even if you did survive and have a long playing span, what awaited you once it was time to hang the boots up. But nonetheless, it was one heck of a great way to live—by playing football.

'I was lucky. I played for what I considered was the best club in the world. I played with many of the greatest players in the game and had some fabulous times. I have made good friends with not only former team-mates at City but across the road at Old Trafford. Because although we loved nothing better than to stuff United in a derby, once the game was over we were the best of pals. I was particularly proud to have a warm and close relationship with so many former greats and especially their manager, the one and only Matt Busby, sadly now passed on.'

During the '50s, Barnes stamped his master touch on the team with some stirring midfield performances that are remembered today with enthusiasm by all those who watched them. But little do those City supporters know that Ken Barnes very nearly left Manchester City after playing one solitary first-team game for them. It is a story known only to a handful of players close to Barnes during his early playing days under the managership of that dour Scot Les McDowall.

The young Barnes had been signed at the age of 21 from Stafford Rangers. He was a beautiful passer of the ball, with a flair for attacking football and was a tough tackler as well. An excited Barnes made his first-team début on 5 January 1952 against Derby County, at Maine Road. City won 4-2 thanks to a couple of goals from Johnny Hart and two more from the colourful Ivor Broadis and Welsh international winger Roy Clarke. Barnes was thrilled to have made it into the big time at last. Favourable remarks about his play from many people at the club convinced him his playing career was about to take off. Yet, amazingly, it was to be two and a half seasons before Barnes would again pull on a first-team shirt.

'For some unknown reason the manager McDowall didn't seem to think I could do a good job in the first team,' recalls Barnes. 'So I spent the rest of that season in the reserves and the whole of the next season as well. I became terribly despondent and eventually I could stand it no longer. I went to see McDowall and said that as it seemed he didn't rate me as first-team material could I have a transfer?'

The request was met only with an aggressive reaction by McDowall. For a time after that young Barnes found he wasn't playing in any of the City teams. Eventually, he was restored to the 'A' team and then won his way back into the reserves. But there was silence regarding his transfer request.

'Then I bumped into George Hardwick, the former England full-back, who was then manager at Oldham Athletic,' reveals Barnes for the first time ever. 'He said that he had bid £3,000 for me. I was amazed because that was a big fee indeed in those days—especially for a reserve player. But McDowall had told Hardwick that it wasn't big enough. I was sick. It seemed that I couldn't get a proper chance with City, but at the same time I wasn't to be given the opportunity to show what I could do with another club. Had City accepted the Oldham bid, I would definitely have signed for them and it would have been the end of me with Manchester City.'

So Barnes's long wait in the reserves continued right up to the 1953-54 season. Yet he was far from giving up the fight to show what a talented player he was. During the latter part of that season Barnes and a little known player, Johnny Williamson, had drawn up a deep-lying centre-forward plan in the reserve side. It produced devastating results. 'Our team went over 20 games without defeat,' remembers Barnes. The great Don Revie was highly impressed and suggested to manager McDowall that they should try this new system of attacking football in the first team for the start of the coming 1954-55 season. Reluctantly, the manager agreed. But when the first-team sheet went up on the City dressing-room noticeboard there was no Barnes in the team. Ken was crestfallen. Would his chance never come again?

So without Barnes or Williamson, the two originators of the new system, City tried out the new plan in the first game of the 1954-55 season. Revie was the deep-lying centre-forward in that first match at Preston North End. It was a disaster! City crashed to a humiliating 5-0 defeat. McDowall was bemused. But Revie refused to give up on the new system which was based on the Hungarian national team's style of play which had had such compelling success at that time. He still felt they should have another chance to see if it could work as well in the League as Barnes and Williamson had proved it could in the reserves. Revie insisted to the manager that Barnes must be brought into the first team as the prime mover in the new system. Much to his chagrin, McDowall finally agreed that Ken Barnes should get his chance. The patient Barnes finally had the opportunity to prove once and for all what a truly creative player he was in midfield. In their next match, City hammered Sheffield United 5-2, with Revie getting two of the goals. Johnny Hart also scored two and Roy Clarke got the other. The sports pages boomed out the news the next day. The legendary 'Revie Plan' had arrived . . . and so had Ken Barnes. He was a permanent first-team fixture from that day on.

He had arrived in a big way and there were to be rich rewards for the youngster who had such a bitter and cruel introduction to City's first-team scene. For Williamson, the story was not so rosy. For six games in the middle of the season when Revie was injured, Williamson, the co-instigator of the plan along with Ken in their reserve days, got his first-team chance. He also played three other senior games towards the end of the season and scored four first-team goals. But towards the end of the following season he was transferred to Blackburn Rovers. 'Johnny played an important role in City's success during that period because of his role in the plan's development,' says Barnes. 'Unfortunately his first-team opportunity was limited but his contribution should not be forgotten.'

Indeed it shouldn't. For City now started to produce some glorious attacking football with the goals flowing sweetly and the victories piled up. But, most important of all, this up-and-at-them style of attacking soccer rocketed City to two successive FA Cup finals that were packed with high drama and pathos.

Barnes forged a great friendship with Revie from then on. They were both fascinated by the tactics of the professional game and would talk about it for hours. Long after their playing days were over the two big thinkers kept in close contact and even when Revie had built the great Leeds United side, he constantly sought Ken's views and ideas on the game. Often he would talk out a particular problem with Ken. Many a time I would pop my head into Ken's office as chief scout at Maine Road, as I did as a roving football reporter, and would see the two together in deep conversation.

166

'Don was a good friend and a truly brilliant player and strategist,' says Ken. 'The Revie Plan, as it was named, called on Don to operate from deep, coming through to take up an attacking position. I worked the ball through from the midfield. It was a 4-2-4 formation that really baffled the opposing defences of that time. They didn't know what to do because at that time, all centre-halves did was mark up tight on the opposing number nine. But with Don operating from in his own half they were nonplussed. It called for the deep-lying man to do a lot of running, but Revie thrived on it and we all made it click.

'Don was a great passer of the ball. His whole attitude to the game was ultra-professional. He was always very serious before a game. To him, we were going out to do a job of work and he wanted everyone to get it dead right. He was the real perfectionist. He loved the tactics of the game and was brilliant at picking out weaknesses in the opposition. It did not surprise me one little bit when he went on to become so successful as a manager with Leeds United. Don was ahead of his time. A great footballing mind and a good friend to me. You don't meet a man of his calibre very often in the world of football.'

Barnes rates his former team-mate Bobby Johnstone as one of City's all-time greats. Johnstone was signed from Hibernian in March 1955 for £20,700 and his dazzling displays with City won him four Scottish caps to go with the 17 he gained with Hibs. The tricky Johnstone, with his thick, jet-black hair sleeked back, was a tremendous hit with the crowd. Here was a great entertainer whose control of the ball was spellbinding. 'He hadn't the engine of Colin Bell,' recalls Barnes. 'But he had such magic and skill. He had a great appreciation for the finer points of the game. In his day Bobby was second to none. To see him ease his way past opponents was breathtaking even to his team-mates playing alongside him. He could lick people without even touching the ball, simply by feigning to pass or by a deft movement of his body. Bobby had a talent that was simply pure class. You can't learn to play like that. You can't be taught to play like that. It is simply that you are born with an ability that is unique.'

Barnes has a happy memory of Bobby turning up for a match the day after New Year's Day looking the worse for wear after a night of celebrating. 'He looked white as a ghost and asked me if I had any aspirins as he had a terrible headache from the night before. I

167

told him he must have been mad to go celebrating on the night before a match. But he just pleaded with me to keep quiet about it,' laughs Barnes. 'He took some aspirins. But when we were shooting in before the kick-off he was still complaining of his headache and didn't look fit enough to play a game of cards never mind football. But I need not have worried. We beat Portsmouth 4-1. Bobby got a hat-trick and they were all headers! We didn't half pull his leg in the dressing-room after the match. We suggested he go on the town on the eve of every match in future!'

City's skipper when Barnes got into the side was the iron man of the midfield Roy Paul. The thick-set Paul had an indomitable spirit and was renowned for tackling which left opponents feeling as if they'd got caught in a tank trap. Paul had come from a tough background, being a former coal miner from the Rhondda Valley. He had joined City from Swansea Town in 1950 for £19,500. He won 33 Welsh caps and his power and leadership played a major part in getting City to those successive FA Cup finals in 1955 and 1956.

'He was a tigerish defender,' remembers Barnes. 'Utterly fearless and had two good feet. Okay, Roy was no Glenn Hoddle but he was a sweet passer of the ball. Most of all he was a great leader. He really inspired you out there and when things were getting tough then Roy loved it. He was always in the thick of the battle. We never forgot what he said in the dressing-room when we were all so down after losing 3-1 to Newcastle United in the 1955 FA Cup final. He bellowed at us, "We'll come back next year and we'll win it this time. I promise you." He really meant it. And we did, of course, by beating Birmingham City 3-1.'

Manchester City have been renowned for producing some of the greatest goalkeepers in the game. Top of the tree is the immortal Frank Swift, who sadly lost his life in the Munich air crash in 1958 whilst covering a Manchester United European Cup-tie for a national Sunday newspaper. But many people argue that former German paratrooper Bert Trautmann was every bit as good. Ken Barnes is one of those who holds that opinion very strongly.

Feelings were still running high when Bert arrived at Maine Road to replace Swift when the fans' goalkeeper hero retired in 1949. Trautmann had been a POW and after the war decided to try his luck in English football. Although the Second World War had been over for four years, a section of the City fans were not too happy to think that a German who had fought against us was now being

168

given the accolade of following in the great Swift's footsteps. But Trautmann was a special sort of sportsman and he was quickly made welcome through his superb goalkeeping displays and by his genial manner.

Barnes told me, 'I arrived at Maine Road when Swift was still in action. Although I never played in the same team, I was there to see him in action from close up, both in practice matches and in League games. He was terrific. I have seen many other great goalkeepers like Merrick of Birmingham City and Ted Ditchburn of Tottenham Hotspur during my playing days. I have been able to see the other great goalkeepers up to the present day. I'm talking about people such as Gordon Banks (Stoke City), Peter Shilton (Leicester City), Harry Gregg (Manchester United), Pat Jennings (Spurs), Ray Clemence (Liverpool) and others. But all I can say is that if there was anyone better than Bert then I have yet to see him. His reactions were utterly fantastic and his bravery second to none.'

Trautmann's bravery was never better illustrated than in the 1956 FA Cup final against Birmingham, whom City beat 3-1 to take the trophy. In the second half of the game, Trautmann made a breathtaking save by diving at the feet of Birmingham forward Murphy. He injured his neck. Although no one knew it at the time, he had broken a small bone in his neck and a further blow in that area could have had horrific consequences. Trautmann became the hero of the hour as City celebrated that great FA Cup victory.

Certainly, Trautmann was immensely proud of the role he was playing in English football. He revelled in being the goalkeeper with a club of such distinction as Manchester City and he showed a fierce loyalty to them that I witnessed, along with Barnes, on City's pre-season tour in Germany, in August 1959. City played the German side SC Tasmania 1900 in the Olympic Stadium, Berlin. What started out as a friendly quickly turned into a full-scale battle. Urged on by a fanatical Berlin crowd, the Germans gave City some real rough treatment. In the second half a tremendous storm broke with thunder and lightning turning the scene into a sort of sporting Wagnerian opera. One vicious tackle was too much for Billy McAdams, City's no-nonsense Northern Ireland international striker. He had already been hacked down so he retaliated and was sent off to screams of delight from the home fans. But City won the match 2-1, to the delight of several hundred British servicemen in the crowd. As Trautmann was leaving the field there was an angry exchange of words between him and many of the fans. Then when a German FA official rose at the after-match banquet to make his speech he laced his address with sarcasm and bitterly insinuated that it was City who had started the nasty stuff. With true diplomacy, the City officials refused to react and ignored the jibe. Not Bert, however. He immediately rose from his seat and left the room with a face like thunder. When we press men questioned him outside the dining-hall Bert said, 'Tonight I am ashamed to be a German. I do not want to play in Germany again after what was said in there.' That proved conclusively to every Manchester City supporter and to the rest of English soccer how proud Trautmann was to be a player in our country. It certainly went a long way to helping him become a legend at the Maine Road club.

Barnes reckons Trautmann was the first goalkeeper to set the trend of goalkeepers starting attacks by throwing the ball rather than merely punting it down the field. 'I know other keepers rolled it out underhand. But Bert was amazing by the way he would hurl it a great distance in a style he had developed from playing handball earlier in his career. He would land it at the feet of a man who was unmarked and able to immediately start an attack. We got a lot of goals over the years through those big throws of Bert's.'

Says Barnes, 'Bert's reflexes were absolutely staggering. I have been standing looking back at our goalmouth and seen shots flying in that I thought Bert had no earthly hope of stopping. Yet he would not only hurl himself right across the goalmouth to reach the ball but he would hold it as well. If he was playing today, at his height, he would be worth over £5 million if anyone wanted to buy him.'

Manchester City surprised everybody in March 1960 when they signed a blond-haired Scottish youngster called Denis Law from Huddersfield Town for a then record £55,000. But City had been extremely fortunate to get the lad who was to prove one of the most electrifying forwards in football. Law has revealed to me, 'Arsenal had come in for me before City and Huddersfield Town were happy for them to talk to me. The manager Bill Shankly wasn't happy to lose me. He was a fabulous man. But it was good business for the club to pick up a transfer fee of that size. I naturally fancied the chance of playing for a big club like Arsenal. But when it came to talking terms with me they sent up their assistant manager Ron Greenwood.' It was a bad blunder by the Gunners. Young Law had a lot of pride and he wanted to be sure that the club he moved to really held him in high regard. Not unnaturally, Law decided that if the Arsenal manager, George Swindin himself, could not be bothered to make the trip to talk terms to a player for whom they were willing to break the transfer record then Law didn't want to know. 'I decided Arsenal was not for me,' says Law. 'If the manager couldn't come himself then I didn't want to play for him.'

It was an amazing break for City who were waiting in the wings. Their manager Les McDowall drove over the Pennines and did the deal quickly. Law became a City player. 'I loved the city of Manchester and the football image that it had with this great rivalry between Maine Road and Old Trafford,' says Law. 'It was a hotbed of soccer. I simply revelled in it,' he adds at the memory of his first exciting days with the Blues. But in the summer of 1961, Law went off to taste the thrills of Continental soccer when the crack Italian club Torino paid a massive £110,000 for him—a staggering price for a British player in those days. He returned in August 1962 to join Manchester United for another colourful period in his magnificent career.

'I loved the Italian scene,' says Law. 'I liked the climate, the food, the atmosphere. It was such a thrill. But the tackling you got in Italian football was something else. You just lived in danger of being chopped up in every match. You had to live by your wits. It was murderous the way defenders went for you. But it was no good moaning. It's the way the game was over there. But after one season I felt I had had enough. Had I stayed much longer I could have been put out of the game for good.'

Law's lucky break came when he bumped into the great Manchester United manager Matt Busby after a Scottish international match Law had played in at Hampden Park. 'He asked me how I was getting on in Italy,' remembers Law. 'I told him I was dying to come back to English football so that I could play a proper game again.' It was just the news Matt was praying for. Within a short time, Busby had done the deal and paid £115,000 for Law to come to Old Trafford.

Recalling Law's extraordinary skills, Barnes reckons that although his remarkable goal-scoring performances made him a world-class star at United, the fans never saw the complete artistry Law possessed. 'United supporters never saw his full potential in my opinion,' maintains Barnes. 'Law was capable of a whole range of performances in the team. I had seen him as a youngster at City

when he made my eyes nearly pop out of my head in sheer aston-
ishment at his capabilities. He could be back defending one minute
and then in a flash he was setting up an attack from midfield with
some quite exquisite passing. He even managed to get up and finish
the job off himself. Not only was Denis a dazzling finisher, but he
was a remarkably talented creator. But at United, whilst he was a
thrilling player to watch up front getting those breathtaking goals, I
felt there was so much more to his game than just playing up front—
waiting for a service and sometimes not getting it.'

Ken Barnes vividly remembers playing in a game as player-manager
of Wrexham in the 1959-60 season and seeing a 17-year-old forward
who, even at that early age, had a charisma about his play. It was
young Mike Summerbee playing for Swindon Town. At that point
in his career Mike was on the wing, but he was equally at home
playing centre-forward or striker, as the phrase is in today's game.
While with City he was to be switched from the striker role to the
right wing. Barnes reckons he did both jobs with equal flair and
impact. 'Mike was as good a striker as you could wish to see,' maintains Barnes. 'He could hold the ball up so well and was excellent
with his head. He used to come hurtling up for those high balls at
the far post. But as a youngster, when I first saw him, he was on the
wing. He had something about his game that was rarely seen in
football at that time—he had tremendous guts and determination.
He would go battling back for the ball deep in his own half.

'In the years that followed, and when he came to join Manchester
City and eventually won his way into the England team through his
masterly performances, I used to marvel at the way he would simply
get up with a shrug time and time again after defenders chopped
him down. He had a really big heart. No matter how hard people
used to whack him, it made no difference to Mike. It made him fight
all the harder and he would beat them all the more. He was no
quitter.

'Everyone loved his jokes when he used to do things like putting
a plastic cup on top of a corner flag and balance the ball on it when
he was about to take a corner. But it was the sheer guts of the guy
that I remember most. I particularly remember a really rough match
against Wolves. Both sides were going at it hammer and tongs. Mike
was clattered over the touchline and right into the crowd by a
terrible challenge from a defender. The supporters told us afterwards that Mike had said to them as he struggled over the barrier to

return to the pitch, "Get me back on the park, I'm really going to sort him out." He did . . . by brilliantly making the winning goal.'

Colin Bell ranks alongside football's all-time greats in Ken Barnes's opinion. 'Football followers talk about how brilliant this player and that player are with the ball at their feet or on their head,' says Barnes. 'Yet while Colin could do wonders with a football, it was when he hadn't got it during the game that he still had such a pronounced effect on matters. He used to make some tremendous runs into the box and get into such perfect scoring positions it was quite stunning. Sometimes he wouldn't get the ball. But just by moving in those places in the attack, he pulled the defenders out and made room for other team-mates to score goals. He was an instinctive footballer and the complete team player. Colin had remarkable skill, but beating people with the ball wasn't his particular forte. His magic was the way he could read the game and adapt to any particular circumstance within it. Colin was the epitome of consistency. He knew exactly what was required from him to contribute to the team's success and he did it absolutely brilliantly. If City can start finding players with half the talent of men like Summerbee and Bell then the future will be bright indeed.'

The foremost thing that struck Barnes about Francis Lee when he arrived at Maine Road was the awesome power that his shots carried. 'He was one of the most venomous strikers of the ball I've seen in the game,' enthuses Ken. 'I remember back to my own playing days. There was Dicky Dorsett, of Aston Villa, who had a tremendous wallop. Later, there was Peter Lorimer who was the hot-shot in Revie's exciting Leeds United set-up. At one point they got a machine and timed the speed of his shot which was over 110 mph, making him the hardest kicker in the game at that time. Then of course there was Bobby Charlton, who produced so many famous blockbusters. Just like them, Franny put some beef behind a shot when he had a crack at goal. He caught the ball so cleanly. Yet it wasn't just power that brought Franny so many goals. He was a spontaneous player and had terrific pace, especially over the first six or seven yards that took him past defenders in a flash.

'He was a fabulous character to have around the club. He was always cracking jokes and putting everyone at ease before a tense match. But his greatest quality of all must have been his dogged temperament. Franny was utterly fearless as a player, and to see him going full tilt at defence was to savour the cut and thrust of what real football is all about. He didn't know how to duck a tackle. Winning was everything to Franny. He simply didn't want to know about losing a match. He gave it everything he'd got in every game he played. I know that his infectious spirit will rub off on everybody involved at the club now that he has become the chairman.'

Players are always recalling, with great relish, some of the most wonderful matches of their past, and inevitably they are games which their team won. Yet Barnes especially remembers with a sort of grim fascination and exceptional recall, a battle at Maine Road which City LOST. It was the FA Cup third round replay on 9 January 1957, against Newcastle United following a pulsating 1-1 draw at St James' Park. But if that first encounter had been a thriller, it was nothing compared to the second meeting at Maine Road.

This game kicked off at two o'clock on a bitterly cold day, with sleet periodically lashing the players' faces. But as the epic battle commenced they scarcely felt it. Nor did the 46,900 crowd. Yet after only half an hour's play both the home fans and the dispirited Newcastle fans, who had made the long journey to Manchester, must have thought the game was all over. City were leading 3-0 through an own goal by unhappy United skipper Bobby Stokoe, a neat header by Bobby Johnstone and a third goal from Paddy Fagan. With Newcastle missing their inspiring striker Jackie Milburn, out through injury, there didn't seem the remotest chance of a fightback. Yet the famous FA battlers were to produce a dramatic recovery that must rank as one of their greatest Cup-tie performances.

In the second half there was an astonishing transformation to the game. First Casey scored from a penalty, and then a part-timer for Newcastle, Alex Tait, made it two for Newcastle in the 75th minute. With only three minutes left, Curry headed a shock equaliser to send the United fans crazy and leave the City supporters feeling numb. So the game went into 30 minutes of extra time which were to prove every bit as dramatic as the previous 90 minutes. City lifted their game yet again despite the shock of being pegged back after seeming to have the tie in their pocket. That magnificent Scottish striker Bobby Johnstone cracked home a great goal to give them a 4-3 lead. But once more those amazing Geordies hit back when the darting Len White intercepted a City back pass and equalised. Then, with only two minutes left, White pounced for Newcastle's amazing winner to send the United fans crazy. Yet with the very last attack of the game Dyson seemed to save City with a net-bound strike, only for the ball to come back off the post.

Former *Daily Express* sports sub-editor Keith Donnelly stayed for the whole thrilling encounter, unlike a host of City fans who were complacent that City had made it long before the end. He recalls the game vividly. 'About a thousand or so City fans had left the ground halfway through the second half when City were leading 3-1, believing it was all over,' he says. 'I remember a chap coming out of a shop in Oldham Street, and he saw a fan walking just ahead of us with his blue scarf on. He said he had had to leave the tie early and asked the final score. When the fan said 5-4 he remarked that Newcastle must have made a great fight of it then. But you should have seen his face when he was told that Newcastle had won!'

Barnes ruefully remembers the City dressing-room at half-time during that extraordinary battle. 'There was no way we had relaxed,' he says. 'In fact, we were telling one another that we must keep the pressure on Newcastle because they had that reputation as Cup battlers who came back from the dead. It was just the rub of the green that went their way. But it was an amazing match to be involved in. Had they won 1-0 the game would have been forgotten a few weeks later. Sure, it was a real sickener to lose. But remembering that we had been to the two previous successive FA Cup finals and had won the trophy the previous season by beating Birmingham City 3-1 we couldn't be too downcast. Cup matches prove that old adage, "Football is a funny old game."' He can say that again! For in the fourth round, Newcastle United seemed to have a walk-over tie when they were paired with Third Division Millwall, yet they crashed out of the competition, beaten 2-1. 'We were proud to have gone out in that thriller at Maine Road rather than against a minnow from the lower divisions,' maintains Barnes.

CHAPTER NINETEEN

TOP MANAGERS like the wonderful Sir Matt Busby of Manchester United, the sagacious Joe Mercer at City, the unforgettable Bill Shankly of Liverpool all used to say that it was not just a player's skill that made a great team, but their character. Well, there certainly are some wonderful characters to be found in Mercer and Malcolm Allison's magnificent sides. In signing Colin Bell from nearby Bury, Joe and Malcolm had captured for the club a talent that was to prove every bit as exciting as they were forecasting. When Mercer splashed out the £45,000 Bury wanted for Bell in March 1966, he was a little unsure of just how good a player they had signed. It had been Malcolm Allison who had pressed hard for the club to sign him. But it wasn't long before a delighted Joe was comparing Bell to one of City's greatest ever players—the genius called Peter Doherty.

The flame-haired Doherty graced Maine Road from 1936 until he was transferred to Derby County in December 1945. At the Baseball Ground this richly talented Irish international forward linked up with another all-time great, England's sleek forward Raich Carter. But in his time at City, Doherty produced a host of utterly unforgettable displays. He had an instinctive footballer's brain, could beat defenders with a shrug of his shoulders and a twist of the hips, leaving them looking like petrified statues. Watching him as I did as a schoolboy, it was difficult to imagine there ever being a player to compare to that prodigious talent. But Mercer, who had played with Doherty, was more than capable of drawing a comparison and he said after Bell joined City, 'Bell is the nearest thing to Doherty I have seen.'

Yet it is really a minor miracle that Bell ended up at City at all. When he was an unknown 17-year-old in his native County Durham, Bell was invited first by the mighty Arsenal and then by nearby giants Newcastle United for trials. Luckily as it turned out for City, Bell had sprained his back in the trial at Highbury and could hardly run. 'I really shouldn't have played in the match because of that injury,' says Bell. 'The Arsenal manager Billy Wright had watched me and told me not to bother coming back. You couldn't blame him. But in a way, I wasn't too bothered for there were a lot of clubs showing interest. I had a trial with Newcastle. At first they didn't seem interested. But later they watched me again. When they did come back and wanted me to sign, I wasn't bothered. I had already decided to join another club that really suited me down to the ground.'

High-fliers Newcastle United and the likes of Wolves, also still keen to sign the smooth-moving youngster with such wonderful control, must have been open-mouthed in disbelief when they heard that the club was little Second Division Bury. So what was the attraction of a humble Lancashire club against the likes of Newcastle and Wolves?

'It was quite simply that the people of Gigg Lane were so homely,' says Bell. 'I loved the way they felt, that the simple things of life were important, like asking me if I'd have a cup of tea and then putting the kettle on in the little office,' says Bell, smiling at the recollection. 'They made me feel so welcome. I felt that I could really play well there because I knew I would feel happy about things.' But although it meant that Bell would be travelling far from his native County Durham, he was still made to feel very close to home as the Bury manager who signed him was that famous Geordie and former Newcastle United captain Bobby Stokoe, one of the best central defenders to turn out at St James' Park. Stokoe knew that he had in Bell one of the finest young players he had seen in years.

Ironically Bell made his début for Bury against City at Maine Road, on 8 February 1964, the game ending in a 1-1 draw. He was only 17 and a great career had begun. His exceptional skill rapidly began to emerge and by March 1966, many clubs were sending their scouts to Gigg Lane. Bell was clearly a wanted young man. Allison pushed manager Joe Mercer into getting the £45,000 needed to sign Bell and City had landed a player who was to quickly emerge as world-class—and cheap at the price. 'I had walked into a wonderful club full of the nicest people you could wish to meet,' says Bell. 'It wasn't only that Joe and Malcolm had got a lot of really great players together. They were all super people. It was just like one big happy family. Sure, there would be times when the tension showed and people would snap at one another. But that's how it is in the heat of the game. But once the match was over, everything was forgotten. It was a fun club.

'With people like Franny and Mike Summerbee about there was no end to the laughs. But there was so much confidence in that Manchester City of the Mercer era. Joe was like a father to everybody. He always had a grin and a joke. But he also provided a shoulder to cry on when anyone had a problem. And every player knew they could rely on Joe to listen to any worry they had, no matter how big or how small.

'Malcolm Allison was different. Malcolm was wild, exciting and the most brilliant motivator as a coach that you could find in football. Malcolm would use every trick and ruse to get the best out of us. But, boy, could he inspire us!'

The magnificent career of Colin Bell speaks for itself when you consider that he played over 490 matches for City, scoring 152 goals, and was capped 48 times for England. But just think how much more there was to come from this player of exceptional standards but for the cruel injury which virtually finished his career at only 29 years of age. That tragic blow came in the derby match with United. It was the fourth round of the League Cup on 12 November 1975, at Maine Road. Bell was attacking with the ball just near the edge of the United penalty area. Says Bell, 'I remember looking up and realising I had three options as Martin Buchan came across to challenge me. I could have had a shot. I could have passed or I could try to put the ball past him. I decided on the last option and I have wondered ever since what would have happened to my career if I had chosen one of the other two options.'

Unfortunately, fate had decreed he would try to beat Buchan. The United skipper caught the back of Bell's knee. 'The trouble was I was standing on the leg he made contact with while trying to drag the ball past him with the other. I had all my weight on it when it took the force of the impact and there was no way it would give. When he made contact, the leg bent backwards and ripped both the cartilage and the ligaments and there was blood behind the knee. I knew at that instant in time that this was a serious injury. It was one of those things. The bitter irony was that I was playing in a purple patch. I felt my form had gone off a little earlier on that season. But now I had all my confidence back.'

Bell was stretchered off and Ken Barnes who was present at Bell's side remembers, 'It was a real tragedy. You get to know instinctively in professional football when an injury is a really bad one and Colin's certainly was. You hope and hope, but the game can be cruel.' Even though that match has such bitter memories for him, Bell still manages to joke about it. 'When I went off it was quite early in the game and there was no score. We ended up winning 4-0 so I didn't think they missed me,' he smiled. Bell stoically tried to battle back and did spend a lot of time in the reserves at one point. 'But I knew in my heart when I was playing with some youngsters in the reserves when we won the Central League championship that I wasn't the same player because of the leg. I even played 31 matches in the first team. But the injury was still holding me back. I suppose for any player at that age, it is desperately hard to have to face up to the fact that it is the end of the road.

'I know I kept hoping I could make it. But I think the moment when I had to face the truth came when Malcolm Allison just took me on one side quietly and said, "Colin, don't you think it might be time . . ." He didn't complete the sentence, but I knew what he was saying. So that was it. But I felt a large part of my life was over. I was lost for a long, long time. I didn't know what day it was because before I used to pace each week carefully leading up to the game on Saturday.'

So the brave Bell left the Maine Road playing scene which he graced so superbly for nine years. However, he plays a part-time role on the coaching staff. But Francis Lee and Mike Summerbee, who linked so magically in that City team with Bell, both reckon City lost out as badly as the luckless Bell when he collapsed in agony in that derby match. 'He was only 29 and would have played for at least another five years,' says Lee. 'It was tragic and City lost a great player whose talent was irreplaceable,' Summerbee agrees. 'Colin was the type of player who would have gone on playing at the top for at least another six years or so. He had a prodigious talent. Colin was effortless and it was a joy to play in the same team as him.'

Bell reckons he could have gone on as his two former team-mates say. But he takes a brave and philosophical attitude to his terrible misfortune. 'Obviously, it was a heck of a blow at the time. But I like to think that I was lucky it didn't happen a lot earlier in my career. There are many, many great young footballers whose chances were brought to a sad end much earlier in their careers than happened to me.'

Then he added, 'I like to remember how lucky I was to end up in that great team with all those wonderful lads. What a bunch they were. It was a great time for the laughs and for the thrills of winning what we did. When we won the championship it was a terrific kick because, remember, there were a heck of a lot of top teams fighting us for it like Manchester United, Liverpool and Leeds United. But I'll tell you why I think that team was such a great one. Although the media used to pick out individuals like skipper Tony Book, Franny Lee, Mike Summerbee and myself as stars, it wasn't like that in the dressing-room or on the field. The real success of that Manchester City team was that nobody was better than anybody else or thought they were.'

Showing a Manchester United shirt to City's fire and brimstone midfield man Mike Doyle is like showing a red rag to a bull. So no one's chest swelled with greater pride than his when they lifted the League Championship in the 1967-68 season and followed up with a string of glittering trophies. 'At long last we had shown that we were the number one football club in Manchester,' says Doyle with obvious satisfaction. 'I had had United rammed down my throat ever since I had been a kid at school. It had been a dream for me to have played in the City team that finally pushed United out of the top spot after so many years.'

Doyle's father was a policeman and a rabid City fan. He implored his son to sign for the Blues as a teenager. But there were plenty of clubs after him—Everton, Wolves, Stoke City and, yes, you've guessed, Manchester United. 'It was the City scout Harry Godwin who swung it as far as I was concerned,' recalls Doyle. 'He made no wild promises but just explained why he felt my future would be in better hands at Maine Road than anywhere else. He was the last of the clubs to approach me. But I decided that City was the spot for me. My dad was over the moon.'

So the dynamic Doyle was destined for Manchester City. But despite his love of Maine Road and his feeling of antagonism towards Old Trafford, Doyle insists United have a fabulous record and is the first to admit it. 'I am the first to acknowledge that Matt Busby had done a brilliant job and built some terrific United teams. But we all felt at City that it was time the Blues showed what they could do. I think the greatest thing about the Joe Mercer team was that it played with such style. We attacked and never feared anyone. The fans loved the class and dash of the team. To beat United is especially gratifying to me. Those victories were truly sweet, I can tell you.'

Yet despite his fierce rivalry with United, Doyle had plenty of friends in the Old Trafford camp—especially defender Bill Foulkes. Looking back, he remembers one of the biggest surprises in his City playing days. 'It was the arrival of Malcolm Allison and the first day he took over the coaching. It was at the training ground. We didn't quite know what we were in for from the huge bloke in the track suit. But we certainly found out in double quick time. After he had watched us going through our paces for a short while he blew his top. He told us we were a lazy lot of so and so's and things were going to be different from now on.

'They certainly were! He really put us through it. But it was different and it was stimulating. We knew it was going to make us better players and turn us into a far better team. Malcolm was really something. No wonder Joe Mercer had that grin on his face when Malcolm had got through with us on that first day of training. He knew he'd picked the right coach!'

CHAPTER TWENTY

FRANCIS LEE has triumphed. After five months of unrelenting struggle for control, he has stormed to power at Maine Road, the scene of some of his greatest performances as a mercurial striker. During those champagne days of Joe Mercer and Malcolm Allison, Lee and his exciting playing colleagues of the '60s brought a pile of glittering trophies to the Maine Road boardroom. They won the League Championship, the FA Cup, the League Cup, the European Cup Winners Cup and the Charity Shield which they won with a record 6-1 score.

So now that Lee and the astute, silver-tongued ally Colin Barlow, another explosive ex-City winger, are ensconced in the Maine Road boardroom, what will the future hold for the restless, hungry City fans? They have waited nearly 20 years for success. In all that time, City have won only one trophy—the League Cup, under former skipper Tony Book's managership. But can chairman Lee and chief executive Barlow turn it round? They know they will be under tremendous pressure to bring back the glory days they have promised the supporters. They fully realise that whilst those fans are throwing flowers in their victorious path after the boardroom battle, there will be flak to follow if Lee and Barlow don't produce the top-quality football they have been craving for so long.

'What we need most of all at the outset is patience,' Lee tells me. 'That goes for me and Colin as well as the fans. We have to realise that we cannot possibly charge in and start changing everything overnight. We have to take stock and talk to people and listen to what they have to say. Those City supporters have been quite unbelievable in their loyalty to the club over such a long, barren period. It has been especially galling for them in more recent years to see Manchester United across the road giving their manager millions and millions of pounds to buy the very best players, thus enabling United to win the championship and put them right at the top of English football.'

One thing that has helped Lee in his battle to take control at Maine Road has been the unstinting support of all his old colleagues of the magnificent Mercer days. No one has supported Franny more completely than ex-City forward Mike Summerbee, that former sorcerer of the wing who used to bewitch a packed Maine Road ground week after week with his spells of pure magic. Summerbee's confidence that Lee's new régime can transform City to a really prominent football place is unshakeable. 'His soccer knowledge is exceptional,' says Mike. 'As a player he always assessed a game and the opposition with an expert's view. And just look what he has achieved in the world of big business. You don't become a multi-millionaire like Franny has done without having an exceptional brain for high finance and a tremendous knowledge of your business subjects. He is also extremely accomplished at handling people. He has a great way with people and a marvellous sense of humour. In short, he is a leader of the highest quality who knows both his football and the way a big club should be run.'

Lee wants the best for City—that's for sure. For too long City have gone for stop-gap signings. There have been times when they have splashed out big money. Yet again, many have never measured up by proving the worth of their enormous cost. But Lee is determined City must have the best. 'When Manchester City go for a player now it will be the best—someone with a top pedigree who will produce the quality football needed to help build a winning side. No more short cuts like in the past. Only the very best will do.'

So Lee and Barlow embark on an exciting new chapter in Manchester City's fascinating history. The past 20 years have been plagued by enormous set-backs that often seemed quite extraordinary . . . almost eerie. Yet when you recall the story of what happened when City first decided to move to Maine Road from their old Hyde stadium maybe it's not so surprising!

Certainly, the arrival of Lee in the boardroom is going to give the club a fresh hope and a confident outlook. Who better to assess the failings in the past and his hopes for the future than former City chairman and director Eric Alexander? The Alexander family has played a proud role in City's history. Eric's grandfather Albert Alexander Senior was a founder and vice-chairman of the club. His father Albert Junior was chairman before Eric. It was in April 1983 that Eric Alexander created high drama at Maine Road when he resigned and spoke out boldly against the way the club was heading. In his opinion, Eric Alexander felt the business side of football and the making of money was being put before the game of football itself. 'I am one of the guilty men,' he said at that time. 'There are many of us. Players, managers and directors as well, caught up in an unhealthy situation which has now made finance more vital than football. That is why I must, with great sadness, quit a club which my father and grandfather have been involved in for so long. Between us we have a longer association with one club than any other family in the country. Between us, particularly my father and myself, we were there during the successful years of City when the club was popular and respected throughout the country—at a time when it was the players who received the publicity. Today egos have inflated. Everyone, it seems, wants to get in on the act and into the headlines, into the sports pages or television. This chase for popularity, for top-dog status has led clubs all over the country into tragic financial commitments, expenditure which exceeds their income. City have been one of the front-runners in heavy expenditure, and as a director of that club I have to accept my responsibility.

'People say that at some clubs there is virtually one man running things, but that has been the case in football from time immemorial. You can quote instances of this all over the country. A small shareholder, even with director status, has little say in the running of a club. But the important thing at any club where you have a principal shareholder in charge is the type of individual he is and his attitude to football. There is the probability of a big new share issue coming up.' (City offered £450,000 worth of new shares on a nine for one basis.) 'It is obvious that the club will want on its board, men willing and able to take up those shares. As I have told the chairman Peter Swales, I do not feel able to do so and accordingly feel it is up to me to resign and make way for someone who is willing to do so. It has been an amicable arrangement. Reference has been made to disagreements over some things. Certainly there have been actions in the past with which I disagreed. It would have been nice to have had more say in the financial spending, but it is natural that those persons with the major money commitment should have the primary say.'

These were words that carried an ominous message for City fans. Eric Alexander felt that men who knew very little about the footballing side of the game were now in control of the club and guiding it the wrong way in the wrong manner. Alexander certainly knows his soccer. He was a talented amateur who played locally. He had always prided himself on his soccer knowledge and felt his prime use as a director to the club was his expertise about football. 'I was never one for the financial aspect really,' he added. He was given a life vice-presidency but this was mysteriously withdrawn some years later, as were several other vice-president positions. But Alexander quit the board with honourable words echoing down the Maine Road corridors of power when he said as he left the club's powerhouse, 'It is the end of the Alexander era! It is not a decision I have taken lightly. I cannot deny the very great sadness I feel in leaving the board of directors. But I believe this move is in the best interests of the financial future of Manchester City Football Club. And, at the end of the day, that is all that matters.'

Then came the final message to the supporters who must have been shocked to hear of the end of the Alexander association with their great club. 'It really doesn't matter if I go or if the chairman quits, so long as City survives. This is my sad contribution to that end.'

If Alexander was depressed at the bleak future he rightly forecast for City on that sad day, he is bubbling with excitement at the thought of the new régime under Lee's hand. 'Franny has always been an out and out winner,' says Alexander. 'He has such wonderful fighting qualities. He showed those on the pitch as a player—he never knew when he was beaten—and he has shown them in his world of business. He has always succeeded in anything he has taken on. The future for Manchester City could not be in safer hands. I believe he has great vision and will transform the club's fortunes on the field at long last.'

Alexander recalls the joy it was to deal with Franny regarding a new contract in comparison to other players. 'Most players would haggle for hours over the most minute details and could drive you up the wall,' says Alexander. 'But Franny was fabulous—a breath of fresh air. He was so straight—no nonsense. He would settle the whole matter in under ten minutes. He would say what he wanted and then listen to what we were willing to offer. Then he would meet somewhere in the middle without the slightest hassle or argument. Franny is a very big character and as straight as a die. How he kept going when he had those awful business problems quite astounds me after the way he had been knifed in the back. But that is Franny the fighter.

'That's why City are going to be a sure-fire winner now that he is at the helm. He was always utterly forthright in the dressing-room and the only person able to really stand up to Malcolm Allison when he felt Malcolm was over-stepping the mark. And Malcolm would be the first to acknowledge Lee's point. Franny feared no one.'

Alexander salutes Lee's superb battle for fitness. 'He has always had this tendency to put on weight, being a naturally stockily built chap. He loved a few pints when the game was over and he used to joke with me, "The way things are going, I will be square by the time I'm 40." But he always buckled down to his training with a tremendous will and must have been as fit a player as there has ever been on City's books.'